GCSE
Computer Science
Revision Guide

Improving understanding through colour and clarity

Get your FREE digital book!

This book includes a free digital edition for use on a PC, Mac, tablet or smartphone.

Go to ddedu.co.uk/cs-gcse and enter this code...

Code: CSAIU02

GCSE **Computer Science**

Contents

WHAT IS COMPUTER SCIENCE?

Computer science is the study of computing devices and systems and how they work. Computer scientists study the design and performance of computer hardware and software.

THE DIFFERENCES BETWEEN ICT AND COMPUTER SCIENCE

Information and Communication Technology (ICT)

ICT discusses how to properly use computers within an organisation to help solve business problems and meet organisational needs.

An ICT qualification will teach you how to develop and use computer applications to share, store and manage data and/or information.

Topics studied include database systems, programming, networking and telecommunications, information security and assurance, web development and human-computer interaction.

Computer Science (CS)

CS uses theory and science to help create and build usable applications, such as video games, apps and computer programs.

A CS qualification will focus more on the theoretical and mathematical aspects of computing.

Topics studied include software development and design, algorithm analysis, computational theory, object-oriented and systems programming, data structures and computer architecture.

If you enjoy maths and particularly like solving logic problems, then CS may offer you some interesting opportunities.

THE DEVELOPMENT OF COMPUTING TECHNOLOGIES

The use of computing technologies continues to increase in popularity, and along with this, Internet use has grown globally. Today, it is hard to imagine a world without web-enabled smartphones, desktop computers, laptops and tablets.

As a result, the way we access and use the Internet continues to evolve, and this has forced computer scientists to change how they think about computing and programming.

WHAT IS A COMPUTER PROGRAM?

A **computer program** is a sequence of instructions that enables a computer to perform a task; all computing devices need programming in order to work. A program's instructions can be written in a variety of programming languages and then translated into code that a computer can understand. Many new programming languages, such as Python, C++, Kodu and PHP, have been developed to accommodate new uses of computing technologies.

THE USE OF COMPUTER TECHNOLOGY IN SOCIETY

The growth of the Internet and new computing technologies has led to a fundamental change in people's lives at work and at home.

Medical Advances

Advances in monitoring equipment and the use of microprocessors in equipment such as artificial limbs and communication devices have revolutionised medical treatments.

Banking

The introduction of Internet and mobile banking services has given people more instant access to their money and greater flexibility in managing their finances.

Shopping Habits

Online retailers have made shopping at home extremely convenient and because online stores are open 24 hours a day, people can shop whenever they would like.

Social Media

Social media has changed the way we communicate and interact with others. It has also encouraged and enabled people to become more aware of and involved with social and political debates.

COMPUTER SCIENCE CAREERS

New technological innovations and the increasing reliance of businesses and organisations on technology are driving the demand for skilled computer scientists.

Gaining a computer science qualification opens up opportunities in various fields, including information technology, telecommunications, aerospace and defence, financial services, retail, the public sector and charitable organisations.

Popular Jobs for Computer Scientists	🔍 Search	Location: United Kingdom	Your search returned 8 results

Computer Programmer

Salary: £30,000 to £120,000 p.a.

Job description: A computer programmer converts project requirements into code to create and/or modify computer programs. A programmer may also develop instruction sequences.

Responsibilities may include:
- Developing, testing and implementing computer programs for a variety of computer platforms and operating systems
- Writing operating instructions for users
- Developing web-based information systems
- Reviewing and updating programs
- Integrating new functionality into existing applications

Software Developer

Salary: £39,000 to £70,000 p.a.

Job description: A software developer has an important role in the design, installation, testing and maintenance of software systems.

Responsibilities may include:
- Designing software and producing detailed specifications
- Programming test versions of software
- Testing for installation and compatibility issues
- Maintaining systems once they are up and running
- Preparing training manuals for users

Network Engineer

Salary: £30,000 to £60,000 p.a.

Job description: A network engineer installs, maintains and supports computer communication networks within an organisation. An engineer is responsible for ensuring that communication networks operate smoothly.

Responsibilities may include:
- Installing, supporting and maintaining new server hardware and software infrastructure
- Managing email, anti-spam protection and virus protection
- Setting up user accounts, permissions and passwords
- Implementing, maintaining and monitoring network security
- Providing training and technical support for users

Web Developer

Salary: £35,000 to £65,000 p.a.

Job description: A web developer is responsible for the design, layout and coding of a website, as well as its subsequent maintenance and updates.

Responsibilities may include:
- Writing programming code to meet business requirements
- Designing page layouts, graphics and animations
- Registering web domain names and organising the hosting of a website
- Testing websites and identifying any technical problems
- Editing content, debugging code and redesigning web pages

Database Administrator
Salary: £22,000 to £50,000 p.a.

Job description: A database administrator assists with the planning and development of databases and is responsible for database performance, integrity and security. An administrator also troubleshoots any issues users encounter.

Responsibilities may include:
- Monitoring user access and security
- Monitoring performance to ensure fast responses to front-end users
- Mapping out designs for planned databases
- Monitoring available disk storage
- Developing, managing and testing backup and recovery plans

Systems Analyst
Salary: £25,000 to £40,000 p.a.

Job description: A systems analyst designs new IT solutions to improve business efficiency and productivity. An analyst also produces costings for new systems and works closely with clients to implement solutions.

Responsibilities may include:
- Analysing clients' existing systems
- Identifying options for potential solutions
- Writing proposals for modifications or replacement systems
- Ensuring budgets are adhered to and deadlines are met
- Providing training to users of new systems

Game/VR/AR Developer
Salary: £40,000 to £50,000 p.a.

Job description: A game developer is involved in the creation, design and production of games for personal computers, games consoles, social and online platforms, mobile phones and other hand-held devices.

Responsibilities may include:
- Developing designs or initial concept designs, including game scripts and storyboards
- Creating special effects, animation or other visual images
- Participating in quality assurance testing
- 2D and 3D modelling
- Developing and implementing computer programs

Digital Marketing Manager
Salary: £22,000 to £49,000 p.a.

Job description: A digital marketing manager oversees the scope, planning, budgeting, definition and initiation of digital marketing activities.

Responsibilities may include:
- Managing the full digital marketing mix, including website development, email campaigns, pay-per-click (PPC) advertising, search engine optimisation (SEO), blogging and social media marketing
- Working with other departments to plan projects within budget
- Delivering financial reports and sales forecasts to senior stakeholders
- Managing external contractors and in-house staff
- Developing and maintaining effective relationships with key contacts

PROGRAMMING LANGUAGES

Programming languages are required to create the software programs that make a computer work. When a program is being designed, the programmer writes a set of instructions on how the program will work in a programming language.

HIGH-LEVEL AND LOW-LEVEL LANGUAGES

Programmers find it easier to write programs in code that looks more like normal languages; these are known as **high-level languages**. The code details how a problem is to be solved rather than giving instructions on how the computer will provide a solution. High-level language is described as problem-oriented language.

Low-level languages provide instructions on how a computer will execute a program based on how the machine is built. The code will not work on any other type of machine. It is used for programming tasks that are associated with the running of a computer. Low-level language is described as machine-oriented language. Programmers do not tend to use low-level languages for day-to-day programming as they are too complicated and difficult to understand.

COMPILERS AND ASSEMBLERS

A set of instructions written in a high-level language is known as source code. The source code is translated into machine code that a computer can run using a compiler.

Source Code written in high-level language → Compiler → Machine Code

Alternatively, instructions may be written in assembly language. Assembly language uses a set of command words called mnemonics such as LOAD, STORE and ADD. The instructions are specific to the hardware being programmed; different CPUs use different programming languages. Assemblers are used to convert assembly language into machine code.

Assembly Language → Assembler → Machine Code

There are many different **programming languages** that are useful for different tasks. Below are a few examples of different high-level programming languages.

Python

Python is an object-oriented programming language used for websites and mobile applications. It is a popular language because it has a clear structure and is easy to read and understand. Python is used by Google, Instagram and Pinterest.

Logo

Logo is used to control devices. It is often used with a small robot known as a turtle. The turtle can be controlled using logo commands such as FORWARD 50 which will move the turtle forward 50 steps.

Kodu

Kodu was created by Microsoft. It allows users to design and create games on a PC or Xbox. It is a visual programming language that is entirely icon-based. Code icons are linked to form rules that allow the user to define the behaviour of the objects on screen.

C++

C++ was developed from C language to become a more modern programming language providing new features such as object-oriented programming. It is used to power major software programs such as Adobe and Firefox.

Java

Java is an object-oriented programming language created by Sun Microsystems. It is extremely popular and useful for creating web pages and mobile applications. It is designed to work across multiple software programs including Mac OS X and Windows.

Visual Basic

Visual basic is used with Windows to create applications. Windows applications are created using forms with various controls placed on them. Code is created for the controls to produce various results.

Object-oriented programs group data with all the methods (functions) that are applied to that data into one self-contained object. These programs are more reliable, simple and easier to program. Objects can be reused in different contexts within a program or in other programs.

TYPES OF COMPUTERS

A computer is an electronic device that processes data. There are many types of computers, from small, embedded computers, such as those used in watches and calculators, to huge supercomputers that are used to perform computationally intensive tasks, such as weather forecasting.

	General Purpose Systems	Dedicated Systems	Control Systems
Purpose	Programmed to perform a wide range of tasks	Perform a specific function or set of functions	Manage, command, direct or regulate other devices or systems, such as machinery
Features	Can perform multiple tasks, including desktop publishing, sound and video editing, account tracking, email sending and Internet browsing	Have input, output, processing and storage components, but programs are fixed (hardwired) into memory so they cannot be altered	Contain specialised I/O devices, such as sensors, buttons and LEDs to monitor and control devices
Examples	A personal computer, laptop or tablet	ATM, washing machine, autopilot	Fitness monitors, newborn baby incubators, security alarms

NON-EMBEDDED VS EMBEDDED

Non-Embedded computers have a complete configuration of standard components that include hardware, software and peripherals. They are defined by their physical size, speed, processing capabilities, memory size, storage capacity and cost.

Embedded systems are computer configurations in which a processor with limited functionality is built into a larger device to control and monitor the device.

Since embedded systems are created for a single function, they can be engineered for improved performance, durability and efficiency. Therefore, they are usually small, low-cost, robust and very efficient when compared to non-embedded systems.

Embedded systems have become indispensable in a wide range of digital devices from consumer products and household devices to complex systems such as car and aircraft management systems.

MICROPROCESSOR

Multiple chips on motherboard

Data bus

CPU					
General Purpose Micro-processor	RAM	ROM	I/O Port	Timer	Serial COM Port

Address bus

A microprocessor is an integrated circuit that is used to run the tasks involved in computer processing. In a computer system, the microprocessor is the central unit that executes and manages the logical instructions passed to it.

MICROCONTROLLER

Single chip

CPU	RAM	ROM
I/O	Timer	Serial COM Port

A microcontroller is a single integrated circuit that performs a single task. It contains memory, programmable input/output peripherals and a processor, all on one chip.

daydream EDUCATION

CENTRAL PROCESSING UNIT (CPU)

A CPU is a piece of hardware that is responsible for processing data for all the tasks that a computer performs. It is often referred to as the 'brain' of the computer. Without a CPU, you would not be able to perform tasks such as creating a database, writing an email or playing a game.

COMPUTER ARCHITECTURE

Computer architecture refers to the functionality, organisation, structure and implementation of a computer system.

John von Neumann is credited with designing the fundamental concept behind all modern computer systems. Von Neumann Architecture describes a system where a single control unit manages the fetch–decode–execute cycle, and both instructions and data are stored in the same memory unit.

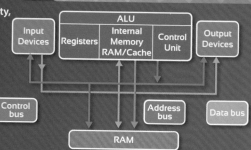

Arithmetic Logic Unit (ALU) – where data is processed, and manipulated. The ALU performs arithmetic and logic operations and comparisons required by the program instructions.

Memory Address Register (MAR) – stores the memory location (address) of the next piece of data or program to be fetched from, or transferred to, memory.

Program Counter (PC) – holds the address of the next instruction to be executed.

Registers – a discrete memory location within the CPU that is designed to hold temporary data and instructions.

PARTS OF THE CPU

Control Unit (CU) – manages the execution of instructions (including the fetch–execute cycle). It also controls the flow of data inside and outside the CPU.

Accumulator – a register within the ALU that 'accumulates' the results of currently running instructions. The final results are then transferred to another register or memory location.

Buses – wires that enable the transfer of data and control signals between the different parts of the motherboard.
The three main buses are:
• Address Bus – carries information about where the data is being sent
• Control Bus – sends control signals to different parts of the computer
• Data Bus – carries the actual data

Memory Data Register (MDR) - temporarily stores the data that is being fetched from, or transferred to, memory. It is also called the Memory Buffer Register (MBR).

daydream
EDUCATION

CPU PERFORMANCE

Processor Cores – the processing components within the CPU. Multi-core processors have multiple processing components within the same CPU.

A dual core processor can process two instructions at the same time whereas a single core processors can only process one. However, this does not mean that dual core processors are twice as fast as single core processors, as processors have different architectures that affect their speed. For example, a processor may require more cycles to complete an instruction than another processor.

Clock Speed – the speed at which a processor operates. The faster the clock speed, the faster the computer will run. Clock speed is measured in hertz: the number of cycles (clock ticks) processed per second.

One clock tick per second = 1 Hz. Therefore a 1,000 Hz processor operates at 1,000 clock ticks per second (1 kHz). A typical home computer has a 3.5 GHz processor that runs at 3,500,000,000 Hz, or clock ticks per second.

Cache - a fast access type of memory that greatly reduces processing time.

It has dedicated connections to the CPU so the CPU has quick access to frequently used data. When the first instruction in a program is requested by the CPU, the other instructions in the program are moved to the cache memory from the main memory to reduce the access time.

Cache memory is expensive so only small amounts of cache memory are present in most computer systems.

GHz

Seconds

Fetch instruction
1. The processor fetches an instruction from the program.

Execute instruction
3. The processor executes one instruction at a time.

Decode instruction
2. The instruction is decoded by the processor.

THE FETCH-DECODE-EXECUTE CYCLE

For a program to run on a computer, it must be loaded into the computer's main memory. The processor locates where the program is stored in the main memory in order to access it.

HARDWARE: SYSTEM UNIT

MEMORY SLOTS

Memory slots are used to connect memory modules, such as the computer's main memory (RAM), to the motherboard. Random access memory (RAM) provides temporary storage for program and data files whilst a program is running. It can be accessed much faster than the hard disk.

Other types of memory that are part of the motherboard include:
Read-only memory (ROM) is a type of permanent memory that stores essential data such as a computer's configuration settings. Once a file has been stored in ROM, a user can read it but not change it.
Cache memory stores frequently used instructions and data in a storage area that is close to the CPU. It can be accessed even faster than the RAM.

ATX POWER CONNECTOR

The ATX Power Connector is used to connect the power supply unit to the internal components of the computer.

THE CPU

The Central Processing Unit (CPU) is responsible for processing data for all the tasks that a computer performs. It uses the motherboard to send and receive signals to the memory and other hardware. The CPU is usually covered in a heat sink to keep it cool.

daydream
EDUCATION

The system unit contains the main parts of a computer system. It typically consists of the motherboard, the central processing unit, internal disk drives, memory, graphics cards and sound cards. A motherboard is a printed circuit board (PCB) that connects most of the other components in the system unit. The other components are either plugged into the motherboard or soldered onto it.

SATA Port

The **SATA port** is used to connect mass storage devices, including the hard drive and optical drives, to the motherboard. The **hard drive** is a computer's biggest memory device; it stores data, programs, and text and media files. **Optical drives** retrieve and store data on optical discs such as CDs, DVDs and Blu-ray discs.

PCI and PCIe Slots

PCI and PCIe slots are used to connect expansion cards, such as graphics, sound, video and Network Interface Controller (NIC) cards, to the motherboard.

A **graphics card** supports the CPU by translating code into images. It also has a processor like the CPU.

A **sound card** enables the input and output of audio signals to and from a computer.

Video and NIC cards are not always required, as they are often built-in to the motherboard.

Ports

Ports enable users to connect peripheral devices to the motherboard.

Devices are commonly connected via the USB, Ethernet, VGA, headphone and microphone ports.

HARDWARE: PERIPHERALS

A peripheral is a hardware device that connects to the central processing unit.
Peripherals are used to provide input, output and backing storage to the computer system.

CENTRAL PROCESSING UNIT (CPU)

The CPU runs computer programs and processes input data into a
readable format understood by humans.

 INPUT DEVICES

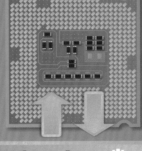

OUTPUT DEVICES

 STORAGE DEVICES

INPUT DEVICES

Input devices send data and control signals to the computer.

Keyboard

A keyboard helps the user interact with the computer. It contains alphabetic characters, punctuation marks, numbers, navigation keys and function keys.

Mouse

A mouse is a pointing device that is used to control the cursor on a computer screen. It enables the user to point at objects and select items.

Graphics Tablet

A graphics tablet is used to reproduce images on a computer screen as they are drawn on the tablet with a stylus.

Touchscreen

A touchscreen is a visual display that a user controls with touch and finger gestures. Smartphones, tablets and touchscreen monitors all use touchscreens.

Scanner

A scanner converts objects and documents into a digital representation that can be processed and edited on a computer and/or printed.

Microphone

A microphone is used to input sound into a computer. The sound can be recorded in a file or processed with voice recognition software.

daydream
EDUCATION

OUTPUT DEVICES

Output devices communicate the results of processed data.

Monitor

A **monitor** provides the main visual display for computer users.

Printer

A **printer** allows hard copies of file content to be created by printing text and images onto paper or other media.

Speakers

Speakers convert the electrical signal from a sound card into audible sound.

Headphones

Headphones convert electrical signals from the device into sounds that can be heard through the headphones.

Lights

Lights, such as light-emitting diodes (LEDs), act as output signals for users. For example, they indicate if Caps Lock is on or if a computer is on standby.

Projector

A **projector** is used to project video output from a computer onto a wall or screen.

STORAGE DEVICES

Storage devices are used to record (store) data.

External Hard Disk Drives

External hard disk drives (HDDs) are high-capacity removable storage devices that are connected to a computer by a port (USB, FireWire, Thunderbolt, etc.).

External Solid State Drives

External solid state drives (SSDs) are high-capacity removable storage devices that use flash memory. They are fast and durable.

Memory Sticks

Memory sticks are small, removable and rewritable storage devices that use flash memory. They are also called pen drives, flash drives or USB sticks.

Memory Cards

Memory cards are used with various electronic devices, such as digital cameras, smart phones and games consoles to store data. They use flash memory.

Optical Storage

Optical storage devices include CDs, DVDs and Blu-ray Discs (BDs). Lasers are used to write data to the discs and read data from them.

Magnetic Tapes

Magnetic tapes are generally used for archiving huge amounts of data. They require a special tape drive for reading and writing data.

MEMORY

Memory refers to the part of a computer system that stores data for use by the central processing unit (CPU). The data includes program files and data files used by programs. The main memory components are situated on computer chips, known as semiconductors. A semiconductor is a material that can conduct electricity under some conditions but not others, making it useful for controlling electrical current.

TYPES OF MEMORY

There are three types of memory:

Volatile Memory

Volatile memory is computer memory that requires a power supply in order to retain stored data. When the power supply is turned off or disconnected, that data is lost. Volatile memory can process data much faster than non-volatile memory. Examples of volatile memory include random access memory (RAM) and cache memory.

Non-volatile Memory

Non-volatile memory is computer memory that can retain stored data whether the power supply is turned on or off. It is used for the long-term storage of files.

Examples of non-volatile memory include read-only memory (ROM), flash memory, hard disks and optical discs.

Virtual Memory

Virtual memory is RAM that is stored on the hard disk to extend the RAM capacity. It is used to store parts of programs currently being run, but the parts of the programs being executed still need to be in the volatile memory.

RANDOM ACCESS MEMORY (RAM)

RAM provides a temporary storage for program and data files whilst the program is running. When you want to use a program, it is loaded from the hard disk (non-volatile memory) to the RAM. If a program were run directly off the hard disk, it would be very slow to respond to your requests.

There are two types of RAM: **static RAM (SRAM)** and **dynamic RAM (DRAM)**. SRAM can hold data without being refreshed for as long as there is a power supply. DRAM needs to be refreshed by frequently reading and rewriting the contents because its stored charge does not last very long. DRAM is more widely used because it is cheaper and takes up less space than SRAM.

daydream
EDUCATION

	Volatile	Non-Volatile	Ability to change data	Access speed
RAM	✓		✓	★★
Cache Memory	✓		✓	★★★★
ROM		✓		★★★
Flash Memory		✓	✓	★

READ-ONLY MEMORY (ROM)

ROM is a type of non-volatile memory that stores essential data such as a computer's configuration settings. Essential data is pre-installed onto ROM chips when a computer system is made. This type of memory is necessary to enable a computer to obtain instructions and information about the hardware from the moment it is switched on. Once a file has been stored in ROM, it can be read but cannot be changed by the user. ROM can be accessed even if your computer has been switched off for months.

FLASH MEMORY

Flash memory is a type of permanent memory that retains data even when the power supply is switched off. It can be changed and rewritten several times. Flash memory is small and portable, so it is being increasingly used in devices such as smartphones, tablets and cameras as well as memory sticks. Flash memory allows faster access to data than a hard disk because it has no moving parts. However, when data is retrieved from external flash memory, such as a memory stick, access speed may be slower as it is restricted by the USB connection.

CACHE MEMORY

Cache memory improves a computer's operating speed by storing frequently used instructions and data in a storage area that is close to the CPU.

Cache memory can be accessed much faster than RAM. Its controllers must predict what data the CPU requires next and retrieve it from the RAM to store in its high-speed memory.

CPU → Cache → Main Memory

17

Secondary Storage

Magnetic Storage

Magnetic storage devices such as hard disk drives (HDD) store data using different patterns of magnetisation.

A read-write head moves across the magnetic surface to detect or modify the magnetisation of the material. A magnetic charge is created in one of two directions represented by either a 1 or 0. As the head moves over the surface the changes in magnetisation are detected and recorded in ones and zeros.

Advantages
- It is capable of storing large amounts of data.
- Data is not lost when the computer is switched off.
- It is a cheap form of data storage.

Disadvantages
- Moving parts make it delicate and susceptible to damage.
- It uses a large amount of power.
- It can be difficult to recover data once damaged.

Cloud

Cloud storage involves uploading data to a remote server or computer via an Internet connection.

Clients pay for online storage space to which they can upload data such as photos, videos, music and documents.

Advantages
- There is reduced risk of physical damage.
- It can be accessed anytime via the Internet.
- It is a secure form of storage – as long as the password is kept private.

Disadvantages
- Basic storage plans are usually free, but larger storage capacities often require payment.
- It can take a long time to upload and download large files.
- Data is at risk of hacking.

Solid-State Drive

A Solid-State Drive (SSD) contains multiple memory chips, which are controlled by software to make them act like a disk drive.

SSDs have no moving parts and are used as an alternative to hard disk drives because of their fast access speed and durability. SSDs use flash memory.

Advantages
- It has a very fast read speed.
- Data is not lost when the computer is switched off.
- It is durable and extremely reliable.

Disadvantages
- Random write speeds of SSDs can be slower than hard disk drives.
- It is expensive per GB stored compared to hard disk drives.
- Some SSDs can be written to only a limited number of times.

daydream EDUCATION

Secondary storage is a means of permanently storing large amounts of data and programs that are not running on a CPU or being stored in the main memory. It is a non-volatile form of storage, meaning that data is retained even when the power supply is turned off, so it needs to be robust and reliable.

Optical Storage

An **optical drive** uses lasers to read and write data on optical discs (CDs, DVDs and Blu-ray discs). To write data, a write laser creates pits (dents) and lands (flat spots) on the optical disc. To read data, a read laser shines light on to the disc. When light hits a pit, it is not reflected; this represents a bit value of 0 (off). When light hits a land, it is reflected; this represents a bit value of 1 (on).

Advantages

- Optical discs can be read by multiple devices such as computers, audio systems and DVD players.
- Data is not lost when the computer is switched off.
- Discs can last a long time if cared for correctly.

Disadvantages

- Data on write-once discs (e.g. CD-R, DVD-R and BD-R) cannot be altered once they have been written on.
- There is a high cost per GB stored.
- Discs are easily scratched, damaged and broken.

Flash Drives and Memory Cards

Flash drives and **memory cards** use integrated circuit semiconductor chips to store data.

Also known as USB or memory sticks, flash drives have no moving parts and are connected to a computer via a USB port. They are commonly used to transfer files and back up data.

Flash memory cards are used with various electronic devices – such as digital cameras, smart phones and games consoles – to store data.

Advantages

- They are small, lightweight and durable, so they are easily portable.
- Data is not lost when the computer is switched off.
- It is easy to access and transfer data.

Disadvantages

- They can be affected by electronic corruption, which makes data unreadable.
- The number of write and erase cycles is limited.
- They are easily lost and broken.

Choosing a Storage Device

Capacity – How much data can it hold?

Lowest				Highest
Optical discs		SSD	HDD	Cloud
	Memory sticks/cards		Magnetic tapes	

Speed – How quickly can it transfer, write and read data?

Slowest				Fastest
Optical discs	Cloud	Magnetic tapes		SSD
	Memory sticks/cards		HDD	

Cost – How expensive is it?

Lowest				Highest
Magnetic Tapes	HDD	Memory sticks/cards	SSD	
	Optical discs	Cloud (often subscription based)		

You will also need to consider how portable, durable and reliable the storage device needs to be. For example, a HDD can be susceptible to damage due to its delicate moving parts, whereas an SSD is tough and hard wearing.

NETWORKS

A network is a connection of two or more computers that enables these computers to share resources and communicate with each other. Networks are vital in modern life. Just look at the world's largest network, the Internet. Could you cope without it?

LOCAL AREA NETWORK (LAN)

- A **LAN** enables the connection of two or more computers at a single site.
- Most LANs include a network file server, a dedicated computer that runs the network software and stores shared files.
- Workstations are connected via wire cables, fibre-optic cables or radio frequencies.
- LANs are often found in offices and schools – places where computers are located on one site.

WIDE AREA NETWORK (WAN)

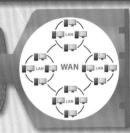

- A **WAN** enables the connection of two or more computers in multiple locations.
- Users are able to access data when they are away from their main workplace.
- Users can connect to a WAN using telephone or ISDN lines, or via a virtual private network (VPN).
- Servers are required for WANs to operate. The Internet is an example of a WAN.

OTHER FORMS OF NETWORK

A Personal Area Network (PAN) is organised around an individual person.

A Virtual Private Network (VPN) uses part of a public network, such as the Internet, to form an extension of a private network.

A Storage Area Network (SAN) connects shared pools of storage devices to multiple servers.

FACTORS AFFECTING NETWORK PERFORMANCE

Bandwidth – Measured in bits per second (bit rate), bandwidth is the amount of data that can be sent or received in a given time.

Number of users or devices – Too many users or devices on a network can slow the network if there is insufficient bandwidth for the data being transmitted.

Transmission media – Wired connections have a higher bandwidth than wireless connections, so they are generally quicker and more reliable. Fibre-optic cables also have a higher bandwidth than copper cables, so they perform better.

Network Topology – The infrastructure of a network can affect its performance. For example, substandard or poorly configured hardware will perform less effectively.

CLIENT-SERVER NETWORK

A Client-Server Network uses designated computers (servers) to serve files and manage services. The client makes requests to the server, which the server then processes and actions. Access to the servers is usually password protected with users having their own login profiles.

Advantages	Disadvantages
Easy to: • Manage security • Manage and locate files • Install software updates • Make backups of shared data	• Expensive to set up and maintain • Specialist IT staff required to set up and maintain • No access by anyone during server downtime

PEER-TO-PEER (P2P) NETWORK

In a Peer-to-Peer (P2P) network all devices (peers) are equal and connect to each other without a server. Each peer serves its own files and is responsible for its own security and backups. P2P networks are often used in the home.

Advantages	Disadvantages
• Easy to set up • No expensive hardware or labour required • No dependency on a main computer (server)	• Not as secure as a client-server network • No centralised management, so backups and updates must be performed individually • Difficult to maintain the file store

WIRED AND WIRELESS NETWORKS

Connections between computers on a network can be wired or wireless.

In a wired network, computers are connected through wires or cables, whereas in a wireless network, radio waves are used to transmit data, so no cables are needed. Mobile phones and televisions also use radio waves to transmit data.

Wi-Fi is the standard used for wireless networks.

Wireless Advantages	Wireless Disadvantages
• No cables or wires required • Network access is available anywhere if a user has a Wi-Fi connection • Relatively cheap to setup • Easily expanded	• Slower than wired networks • Not as stable as wired networks • Prone to interference and obstruction • Vulnerable to hacking

Network Hardware

NIC (Network Interface Controller)

A NIC uses network protocols (usually ethernet and Wi-Fi) to connect a device to a wired or wireless network. It is typically built into the motherboard.

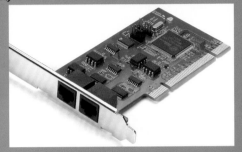

Switches

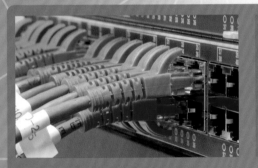

Switches send data between computers on a LAN. They learn which computers are connected and build up an internal index, so data packets are only sent to the correct device or another switch.

Fibre-Optic Cables

Fibre-optic cables use light to transmit data and can cover longer distances than copper cables. They have a higher bandwidth due to reduced interference so are generally used in high-traffic connections.

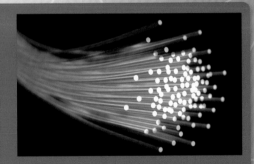

daydream
EDUCATION

To connect to and communicate over a computer network, physical hardware is required.

ROUTER

A router sends data between networks and is needed to connect a LAN to a WAN.

It uses IP addresses to route data packets to other routers and algorithms to determine the fastest route.

ETHERNET CABLES

Ethernet cables are often used to connect devices in a LAN. They consist of four pairs of copper wires, twisted around each other to reduce interference. Usually there is one set of wires for transmitting and another for receiving data.

WIRELESS ACCESS POINT

A wireless access point enables wireless devices to connect to a network without cables. It often includes an integrated router and switch.

daydream
EDUCATION

NETWORK TOPOLOGY

Network topology is the way in which all network components are connected together.

RING NETWORK

Network terminals are connected by a cable in a ring formation.

This network is fast because the data flows in only one direction.

Client 1
Client 2
Client 3
Printer
Server

It is cheap and easy to expand, but it slows down with more users.

This is the simplest network. It is cheap and easy to install.

If the central cable fails, the whole network breaks down.

BUS NETWORK

Each terminal is connected to a single line of cable called a 'bus'.

When one terminal wants to communicate with another on the network, it transmits a broadcast message along the bus.

Client 1
Server
Client 2
Printer
Client 3

If the central cable fails, the whole network will break down.

This is a reliable network because if one connection fails, the others remain unaffected. However, if the central computer fails, the whole network will break down.

STAR NETWORK

It is expensive because it requires a large quantity of cable.

Client 1
Client 4
Printer
Server
(Central computer)
Client 3
Client 2

This is used to connect a large number of terminals to a central computer called the 'central node' or 'hub node'.

If serving many terminals, this configuration will be the slowest.

The central computer controls the network and usually stores shared resources.

Each terminal is connected to the central computer by a separate cable.

daydream
EDUCATION

MESH NETWORK

FULL

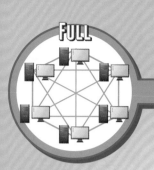

PARTIAL

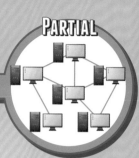

All nodes (devices) are connected, either directly or indirectly, so there is no need for a central switch or server.

Data is sent along the fastest route.

If one route fails, algorithms reroute the data along a different route, in a process called 'self-healing'.

It can be expensive, as all nodes need to be physically connected to each other.

As long as two devices are transmitting and receiving on the same channel, they will be able to communicate and exchange data.

Wi-Fi is a common standard for wireless networks. It uses frequency bands, mainly 2.4 GHz and 5 GHz, to transfer signals, with each frequency band being given a channel number.

Because channels overlap, there is often interference on channels that are close to each other.

WIRELESS NETWORK

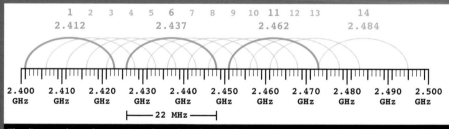

The diagram above shows various channels in the 2.4 GHz range. As you can see channel 6 overlaps with channels 2–5 and 7–10, but it does not overlap with channels 1 and 11. Therefore, channels 1, 6 and 11 would be suitable waveband channels.

It is important to encrypt data on Wi-Fi networks so it is secure. WPA and WPA2 are the main protocols for encrypting data.

NETWORK PROTOCOLS

Network protocols are rules and standards for communication between network devices. Network protocols govern all aspects of network communication from sending and receiving messages to formatting files for different types of messages.

ADDRESSING

A network address serves as a unique identifier for a device on a network.

An IPv4 address
(dotted-decimal notation)

172.16.254.1

10101100 . 00010000 . 11111110 . 00000001

1 byte = 8 bits

32 bits (4 x 8),
or 4 bytes

MAC (Media Access Control) Addresses: Every device on a network has a MAC address, that is assigned to the device's NIC during manufacture. MAC addresses are used to route data (frames) on LANs.

00-5D-BE-80-F4-9A

| Manufacturer Identifier | Hexadecimal digits allocated by manufacturer |

IP (Internet Protocol) Address: IP addresses are used to route data (packets) on WANs. They are generally assigned to a device by the TCP/IP network that is being used. Therefore, IP addresses (called dynamic IP addresses) can change when there is a change in network.

Static IP addresses do not change.

NETWORK PROTOCOLS

There are various protocols in place to make networking possible.

TCP/IP Protocol is made up of two protocols which enable communication between devices.

Transmission Control Protocol (TCP) breaks information down into smaller pieces called packets that allow it to be transported. TCP then puts the pieces back together in the correct order on the receiving computer.

Internet Protocol (IP) is a standard set of rules used to ensure that computers on the Internet send information to the correct address. Every computer on a network must have its own unique address known as an IP address.

OTHER PROTOCOLS

Protocol	Use
FTP – File Transfer Protocol	Used to transfer files from one location to another
HTTP – Hyper Text Transfer Protocol	Used to control the format and transfer of web pages over the Internet
HTTPS – Hyper Text Transfer Protocol Secure	HTTP used over a secure connection on which all data sent and received is encrypted
SMTP – Simple Mail Transfer Protocol	Used to send emails to a mail server
POP3 – Post Office Protocol 3	Used to retrieve emails from a remote mail server
IMAP – Internet Message Access Protocol	Used to manage remote mailboxes and retrieve emails from a remote mail server. It is more advanced than POP3

daydream
EDUCATION

LAYERS

When two remote computers communicate, multiple tasks need to be performed (e.g. digitisation, transmission, routing, and so on). Layering involves organising protocols of similar functions into 'layers' to simplify the overall task.

Layering makes it possible to adjust individual layers without affecting the whole network standard. Protocols can be divided into two parts: logically based (concerning the data itself) and physically based (wired or wireless).

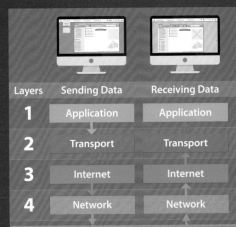

There is a hierarchy of layers, with each layer providing a set of specific functions to the layer below it. Inter-layer communication is achieved through interfaces called Service Access Points (SAPs).

Layers	Sending Data	Receiving Data	Responsible for...
1	Application	Application	Making sure data is in the correct format for the software receiving it
2	Transport	Transport	Establishing connections across the network
3	Internet	Internet	Transmitting data across the network
4	Network	Network	Delivering data to the physical network

PACKETS AND PACKET SWITCHING

When a file is sent over a TCP/IP network, it is divided into packets for routing.

The individual packets travel different routes and are then reassembled into the original file at the receiving device.

Splitting data into packets allows for faster data transfer and a more secure data transmission.

Each packet contains the:

Data Packet
← Packet number
← Sender's IP address
← Receiver's IP address
← Protocol
← Payload (the actual data)
← Checksum number (checks for errors)

Packet switching is used by routers to direct data packets over a network. A routing algorithm is used to determine the best path.

The sending device splits the data into numbered packets.

The routers direct the packets along the best route depending on network traffic.

The receiving device uses the packet numbers to reassemble them in the correct order.

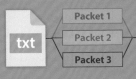

Packet 1
Packet 2
Packet 3

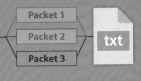

Packet 1
Packet 2
Packet 3

THE INTERNET

The Internet is a system of interconnected networks based around TCP/IP protocol. The World Wide Web (web) is a service that operates through the Internet using http and https protocol.

THE WORLD WIDE WEB

The web is made up of billions of documents, or web pages, that are connected by hypertext or hyperlinks.

Each webpage, written in HTML or XHTML, is stored on a web server and has a unique web address.

A website is a collection of web pages and files. A web browser is required to read web pages.

The Uniform Resource Locator (URL) is the unique address of a webpage.

http://
The data transmission protocol for the web

Domain Name
Used to identify the IP address of a website

/index
Identifies specific pages within a website

http://www.daydreameducation.co.uk/about/

Domain names are used in URLs instead of IP addresses because they are easier to remember.

Domain Name Servers (DNS) translate domain names to their numerical IP addresses, which are needed for locating and identifying services and devices with the underlying network protocols.

Domain Type
.com – company
.co – company
.ac – academic institution
.sch – school
.gov – government body
.org – organisation

Country Code
.uk – United Kingdom
.fr – France
.au – Australia
.de – Germany
.us – United States
.ch – China

Cookies
Cookies are small pieces of data that are created by websites to help identify users so it can prepare customised pages or save login information.

Tabs
Tabs enable users to open multiple web pages within a single window. This is useful when switching between websites.

Bookmarks
Regularly visited websites can be saved using a bookmark. Websites that have been saved can be displayed in categorised lists.

Cookies ✓ Continue ⚙ Change settings ⓘ

Schoogle

Navigating the Web   **GO!**

WEB   IMAGES   MAIL   NEWS   ABOUT

Hyperlinks
Hyperlinks connect to other parts of a site or another website. Hypertext links are usually underlined or highlighted.

Search Engines
Search engines are used to search for websites. Keywords are typed into a search field and related websites are listed.

History
Internet browsers store a list of recently viewed web addresses. The history can be used to find previously visited websites.

---

daydream EDUCATION

HOSTING AND CLOUD STORAGE

Since websites need to serve pages securely to users on a 24/7 basis, they are stored on dedicated web servers. This is known as 'hosting'.

Web servers are also used to store files and for the provision of online software. This is known as 'cloud computing'.

Advantages of 'The Cloud'
- No need for storage hardware
- Easy to share files and collaborate
- Anytime, anywhere access from any device
- Automatic backups

Disadvantages of 'The Cloud'
- At risk of hacking
- Can be difficult to switch providers
- Possibility of web server failure, resulting in downtime and no access
- Necessity of trusting the host with your personal data

VIRTUAL NETWORKS

A virtual network is a network that applies the logic of networking without applying the same physical configuration. Look at the images below.

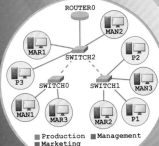

This shows the actual physical layout of a virtual LAN, with partitioning being performed non-physically using software.

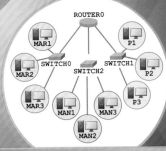

This shows how the virtual LAN would be configured if the logical partitioning was actually performed physically.

Software is used to set user access details so users can only access files that they are permitted to access.

A virtual private network (VPN) uses part of a public network, such as the Internet, to form an extension of a private network so data can be sent securely over a WAN.

Virtual networks are easily scalable and can reduce the hardware required for a network configuration.

SYSTEM SECURITY THREATS

Networks are vulnerable to a wide variety of security threats. Therefore, it is vital to understand, identify and prevent these threats.

DATA INTERCEPTION & THEFT

Data sent over a network is intercepted either directly by a hacker or through software such as packet-sniffing software. Attacks are difficult to detect and are best prevented using data encryption.

DENIAL-OF-SERVICE ATTACK

A denial-of-service (DoS) attack floods a network with meaningless requests or traffic in an attempt to overload its systems, causing it to crash and become unavailable to users.

BRUTE FORCE ATTACK

Trial and error is used to guess information such as passwords or personal identification numbers (PINs). Automated software is often used to generate a large number of consecutive guesses.

Login
Administrator
Password
* * * * 5842

POOR NETWORK POLICY

An organisation should have a security policy that outlines a set of rules and procedures that, when followed, ensure the network is not open to attack.

SECURITY THREATS

SOCIAL ENGINEERING

People are often the weak point in a system. Therefore, many hackers use deception to manipulate individuals into divulging confidential or personal information. Phishing is a type of social engineering.

SQL INJECTION

Structured Query Language (SQL) is a language used in database management systems to perform operations and access data. Malicious SQL script inserted into web forms can program the website's database(s) to provide sensitive information.

PHISHING

Phishing is the practice of persuading an individual to disclose private information, such as bank account details or passwords, usually via email or using a fake website.

HACKING

Hacking is unauthorised accessing of a computer system, often with the goal of stealing data, causing damage or exposing problems.

daydream
EDUCATION

⚠ MALWARE

Malware is malicious software that is installed on a system with the aim of :

- damaging or deleting files
- stealing information
- taking control of the system

✕ VIRUSES

A virus is a program designed to copy itself. It cannot spread without human assistance and is often hidden in other programs.

✕ WORMS

A worm is a self-replicating program that can run itself, allowing it to spread very quickly and exploit weaknesses in network security.

✕ TROJAN HORSES

A Trojan horse is a program that disguises itself as legitimate software and appears to perform one task but actually performs another.

✕ RANSOMWARE

Ransomware is installed covertly on to a victim's device and threatens to cause damage unless a sum of money is paid.

✕ ROOTKITS

A rootkit allows an unauthorised user to gain full control over a computer, including the host operating system, to avoid detection.

PREVENTING SECURITY THREATS

To identify and prevent threats to data, organisations can use:

PENETRATION TESTING

Penetration testing (or pen testing) uses an authorised, simulated attack on a computer system to look for security weaknesses that could enable unauthorised access to the system and its data.

NETWORK FORENSICS

Network forensics are procedures that capture, record, and analyse network events to discover the source of security attacks or other problems.

NETWORK POLICIES

Network policies are rules and guidelines concerning what network users can and cannot do. As well as covering general use, a good network policy should set guidelines for:
• email, web and Internet use
• passwords
• incident reporting
• remote access
• user permissions

ENCRYPTION

Encryption uses algorithms to convert data into ciphertext (encrypted text), that cannot be decrypted without the decryption key.

PASSWORDS AND USERNAMES

Passwords are used to ensure only authorised users can access the system. Different programs may require different complexities of password, as well as different character lengths.

USER ACCESS LEVELS

User access levels control user access rights on a computer system. For example, the owner of a company, is likely to have access to all files on the network, whereas junior staff are likely to be restricted from accessing or editing confidential files or folders.

FIREWALLS

A firewall is a software or hardware security system that controls incoming and outgoing network traffic. Packets of data are analysed to determine whether they should be allowed through or not.

ANTI-MALWARE SOFTWARE

Anti-malware software examines incoming traffic and performs scans to protect from malware infiltration and infection. New malware is always being created, so software needs to be updated frequently.

Your computer is protected

UTILITY SYSTEMS SOFTWARE

Utility systems software supports a computer's infrastructure, helping to configure, optimise and maintain the computer system. Many utility programs are installed with the operating system, but others can be installed by the user to help manage the system.

ENCRYPTION SOFTWARE

Encryption software prevents the unauthorised accessing of data. The software encodes (scrambles) data so anyone intercepting it will not be able to read it. The data can only be decrypted with an encryption key.

DATA COMPRESSION SOFTWARE

Most operating systems are supplied with compression software that makes files smaller by removing redundant data. This is often done so that the files take up less disk space or can be transferred more quickly.

DEFRAGMENTATION SOFTWARE

Files on a hard disk are not stored together in one location. They are broken up into fragments so that they can fit into the available spaces on the drive. As more files are moved, deleted or edited, the disk becomes more fragmented, so it takes longer for the read-write heads on the drive to access all the fragments.

Defragmentation software reorganises all the fragments, so whole files are put back together and all free space is located in one area.

1 User saves new file.

2 The data in the file fills empty spaces and becomes fragmented.

3 Deframentation software puts the fragments back together.

BACKUP SOFTWARE

Backup software creates copies of files, whole drives or entire networks to prevent data loss or damage.

Full Backup

All files are copied to the backup medium.

Requires more storage and takes longer than an incremental backup, but it is quicker to restore as there is only one backup.

Incremental Backup

Only the files created or edited since the last backup are copied to the backup medium.

Faster and smaller than a full backup, but the restore is slow as all incremental files need to be restored.

33

OPERATING SYSTEMS

An operating system (OS) is a collection of programs that controls a computer system's hardware and enables applications and the rest of the system to work.

Operating Systems are found in nearly all computers, from video consoles to mobile phones. Windows, Android, Mac OS and iOS are the most popular operating systems.

User	Application Software	System Software	Hardware
	Internet browsers, word processors, spreadsheets	Operating system, utilities	CPU, disks, peripherals

1 MEMORY AND CPU MANAGEMENT

The OS manages available memory, moving programs and data in and out of memory as and when they are needed. When an application is opened, the OS moves the required parts to memory so they can be accessed quickly by the CPU.

To ensure that the multiple programs in memory are secure and do not overwrite each other, the OS allocates programs and their related data to specific memory addresses.

A multitasking operating system schedules tasks and shares CPU time so efficiently that the CPU appears to be processing several programs at the same time.

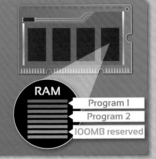

RAM
Program 1
Program 2
100MB reserved

2 PERIPHERAL MANAGEMENT

Device drivers are programs that are installed onto a computer system when a peripheral device is connected to it. These drivers act as a translator between the peripheral device and the applications or operating systems that use it.

Drivers enable operating systems and other computer programs to access peripheral functions without needing to know the precise details of the device.

3 USER MANAGEMENT

Single-user operating systems allow only one user to access a computer at a time.

Multi-user operating systems allow multiple users to simultaneously access a computer. The OS manages user accounts, controlling permissions and access levels to specific locations or resources.

User accounts are often password or pin protected to prevent unauthorised access to and theft of data. Devices may also contain fingerprint or retina scanners.

Username
LOGIN
Remember me   Forgot Password?

daydream
EDUCATION

4 USER INTERFACE MANAGEMENT

A user interface is the means by which a user communicates with an OS and interacts with a computer system.

Command-line Interface

In a command-line interface users type commands to communicate with the OS. A command-line interface begins with a prompt, such as **C:\>**

Commonly used sequences of commands are often batched together in scripts so multiple actions can be initiated using single commands.

A command-line interface can be an efficient way of communicating with the OS as long as the user knows the commands.

Graphical User Interface

A Graphical User Interface (GUI) enables users to interact with the OS through windows, icons, menus and pointers. A GUI is intuitive and reduces the need for users to learn complex commands. However, it requires more RAM and processing power.

Other User Interfaces

Other interfaces include menu driven interfaces, in which commands are chosen by the user from a series of menus, and voice input interfaces, in which voice recognition software interprets and carries out users' spoken commands.

5 FILE MANAGEMENT

Computers store data as files and the OS manages and organises these files so that they are stored efficiently in a hierarchical structure.

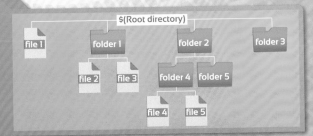

THE OPERATING SYSTEM ALSO...

monitors performance. If the OS is unable to process a command, it alerts the user to the problem	operates utilities to maintain the computer and enable applications to run smoothly	runs virus protection and diagnostic software

daydream
EDUCATION

COMPUTER TECHNOLOGY ISSUES

Computer technology is vital in today's society. However, despite its various advantages, technology also has a wide variety of negative impacts.

PRIVACY

It is difficult to keep information private whilst using technology. When registering for new websites and services, you are expected to accept a privacy agreement and provide personal information that can often be used and shared by the provider.

Computer technology is also used to monitor behaviour. Companies can monitor your behaviour over the Internet and using mobile phone signals. New surveillance legislation forces ISPs and mobile operators to keep a record of every citizen's browsing history for up to a year.

Whistle-blowers are people who expose any information that is deemed illegal, unethical, or not correct within an organisation's policies. WikiLeaks is a website that publishes information from anonymous whistle-blowers.

ENVIRONMENTAL

The use of computers affects the environment in various ways, including the use of finite natural resources, energy consumption and technological waste.

Advantages

Technological advancement has helped with the development of new practices, machinery and devices that consume less energy and natural resources.

Electronic communication, such as email and video messaging, reduces the need for physical mail and travel. This reduces paper usage and pollution due to travel.

Disadvantages

Extraction and use of natural resources used in electronic devices both depletes those resources and causes pollution.

Billions of electronic devices are used daily, requiring huge amounts of energy.

Up to 50 million tonnes of e-waste is generated every year, with many electronic devices containing toxic materials that harm the environment.

HEALTH

The overuse of technology in the workplace and at home can lead to several health issues, such as eye-strain, repetitive strain injury (RSI) and posture problems.

The increased use of technology has also meant that people are spending more time on mobile devices and less time interacting socially. This can have a detrimental effect on people's social well-being and general health.

36

daydream
EDUCATION

ETHICAL AND CULTURAL ISSUES

In trolling, perpetrators known as trolls post offensive or off-topic material online to cause shock or an argument, for example, posting a derogatory comment on a Facebook picture.

The Internet provides anonymity, so people often say and do things online that they wouldn't normally do in person.

Cyberbullying

Cyberbullying is bullying or harassment using electronic forms of communication, such as email, online gaming or social media. It has become increasingly common, especially among teenagers, and can cause huge distress to the victim.

11:30

In sexting, perpetrators trick victims into sending them sexually explicit images or videos so they can share them publicly.

There are no specific laws against cyberbullying, but it can be dealt with under the Defamation Act 2013.

The Darknet

The darknet, a collection of non-indexed websites, is estimated to be 400 to 500 times larger than the surface web of indexed, searchable websites. The darknet has become a conduit for illegal and often dangerous activities.

Darknet

Unequal Access to Technology (the Digital Divide)

Location and wealth affect people's levels of access to technology. With technology playing such a huge role in society as a tool for communication, education, business, and so on, people with limited access to technology are likely to be seriously disadvantaged. It is argued that the digital divide has increased social inequality.

Virtual Currencies

Virtual currencies, such as Bitcoin, provide a low-cost way of exchanging money online without the interference of banks or authorities. The anonymous nature of these currencies makes transactions very difficult to track, and some argue that they facilitate money laundering and the purchase of illegal goods.

THE DATA PROTECTION ACT

The Data Protection Act was introduced in 1984 to deal with the storage and misuse of personal data. It was updated in 1998 with new legislation that incorporated the European Data Protection Directive. The 1998 Act was then updated in May 2018 to include the provisions of the European Union's General Data Protection Regulation (GDPR).

1

The processing of personal data for any purpose must be lawful and fair.

The data subject must consent to the data processing, and the processing of the data must be necessary for the task being carried out.

6

Personal data must be processed in a manner that ensures its security.

This will involve using appropriate technical or organisational measures.

2

The purpose of data collection must be specified, explicit and legitimate. Personal data must not be processed in a manner that is incompatible with the purpose for which it was collected.

5

Processed personal data must not be kept for any longer than is necessary for the purpose for which it is processed.

Periodic reviews must be set up to evaluate the need for continued storage of personal data.

3

Processed personal data must be adequate, relevant and not excessive in relation to the purpose for which it was processed.

If the data is not specifically required, it should not be collected.

4

Processed personal data must be accurate and, where necessary, kept up to date.

Every reasonable step must be taken to ensure that inaccurate personal data is deleted or amended immediately.

THE COMPUTER MISUSE ACT

What is The Computer Misuse Act 1990?

The Computer Misuse Act 1990 was introduced to deal with the increased incidence of computer hacking (the unauthorised accessing of a computer system).

It aims to protect computer users against wilful attacks and theft of information.

Login
Administrator
Password
* * * * 6842

The Computer Misuse Act 1990 Makes It Illegal To:

Gain unauthorised access to another person's software or data.

Gain unauthorised access to another person's software or data with the intention of breaking the law further.

Gain unauthorised access to another person's software or data with the intention of altering or deleting it, including by planting viruses.

Example:

The owner of a business hacks into a competitor's network.

Example:

The owner of a business hacks into a competitor's network to steal data.

Example:

The owner of a business hacks into a competitor's network to copy data and plant a virus.

THE COPYRIGHT, DESIGNS AND PATENTS ACT

WHAT IS THE COPYRIGHT, DESIGNS AND PATENTS ACT 1988?

The Copyright, Designs and Patents Act 1988 provides developers and authors with proof of ownership and exclusive rights to reproduce and distribute their work.

It protects the intellectual property of individuals or organisations, making it illegal to copy, modify or distribute intellectual property without permission.

THE COPYRIGHT, DESIGNS AND PATENTS ACT 1988 MAKES IT ILLEGAL TO:

Use software illegally, thus breaching licence restrictions.

Example:

Someone installs single-user licensed software on multiple computers.

Replicate digital files without authorisation.

Example:

Someone copies a computer game.

Distribute and sell digital files without authorisation.

Example:

Someone places purchased music on a file-sharing website for people to download.

daydream EDUCATION

FREEDOM OF INFORMATION ACT & CREATIVE COMMONS

FREEDOM OF INFORMATION ACT 2000

The Freedom of Information Act 2000 requires public organisations to publish certain data so that the public can access it. It also gives individuals and organisations the right to request official information held by over 100,000 public bodies.

Some of these public bodies include:

Central government, government departments and local authorities

Hospitals, doctors surgeries, dentists, pharmacists and opticians

State schools, colleges and universities

Police forces and prison services

The Act covers information such as emails, minutes of meetings, research and reports. Organisations have the right to withhold information that could cause harm or affect national security.

CREATIVE COMMONS LICENSING

The Creative Commons organisation issues licences that enable copyright holders to grant selected rights to the public to share, use, and/or build upon their work, whilst retaining specified rights.

cc creative commons

The main types of licence are shown below:

Universal (CC0)
Allows free use of the work without restriction

Attribution (BY)
Licensees must acknowledge the copyright holder or author of the work

ShareAlike (SA)
Licensees may distribute the work under the same licence that governs the original work

NonCommercial (NC)
Restricts work from commercial use

NoDerivatives (ND)
Prohibits modifications of and additions to the work

There are also licenses that combine two or more of these types. For example, an Attribution-NonCommercial licence (BY-NC) allows for the work to be used, built upon and shared non-commercially as long as the copyright holder is acknowledged.

Open-Source Software vs Proprietary Software

Open-Source Software

Open-source software is software that is freely available so that others can use it. Users can access and modify the source code to create their own versions.

There are often communities of developers that support and update open-source software, sharing ideas and solving problems to fix any issues and make improvements.

Advantages
- Usually free of charge
- Can be modified to suit users' needs
- Encourages collaboration and innovation
- Collaborators are often quick to fix any problems

Disadvantages
- New releases are often buggy
- More open to security threats
- No official support
- No one is accountable for any problems

Examples
Linux OS, Android OS and Mozilla Firefox web browser are examples of open source software.

Proprietary Software

Proprietary software is software that is not freely available. The compiled code is released as executable programs, so users cannot access or modify the source code.

Copyright laws make it illegal to modify, copy or redistribute the software.

Advantages
- Full support is provided by proprietary software owners
- Usually very secure and free from bugs
- Bugs and other issues are often fixed for free in software updates
- Often includes warranties and user documentation

Disadvantages
- License purchase usually required
- Can be expensive, especially if multiple licences are required
- Users cannot modify the source code to suit their needs

Examples
Microsoft and Adobe are two of the biggest proprietary software developers.

daydream EDUCATION

ALGORITHMS

An algorithm is a sequence of instructions used to solve a problem. Sequence means that there is an order to the instructions.

Computational thinking involves the examining, understanding, formulating and solving of problems. It consists of four main elements.

Decomposition – breaking down complex problems into smaller, easier-to-solve parts

Abstraction – focusing on the main parts of the problem and ignoring specific details

Pattern Recognition – looking for trends and/or patterns in a problem

Algorithmic Thinking – creating a sequence of instructions to solve the problem

System Flow Chart

A system flow chart is a diagram that is used to show the breakdown of an algorithm into steps. Each step is represented by a particular symbol, and arrows indicate the flow of tasks. The symbols used in a flow chart are standardised. Below is an example of a system flow chart for taking a pizza order.

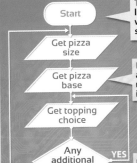

Terminators (shaped like an oval) indicate where the algorithm starts and finishes.

Inputs (shaped like a parallelogram) represent an input action.

Decisions (shaped like a diamond) pose a question and have different routes out for different answers.

Processes (shaped like a rectangle) are actions to be performed, such as instructions and calculations.

Outputs (shaped like a parallelogram: the same shape as an input) represent an output action.

Pseudocode

Pseudocode is an algorithm written in a programming-style construct, but it does not follow a specific programming language. It describes an algorithm using a series of statements. It does not need to include detailed syntax or specify how the code will work. Below is an example of an algorithm for taking a pizza order.

```
Identify the pizza size selected
Identify the pizza base selected
Identify the topping choice selected
IF additional toppings required THEN
    Add to the topping choice
ELSE
    Identify if another pizza is to be added
END IF
IF another pizza is to be added THEN
    Identify the pizza size, base and topping
ELSE
    Calculate order price
    Display order
END IF
```

The system flow chart or pseudocode must be converted into a programming language, such as the examples listed below, before it can be used to perform tasks on a computer.

SORTING ALGORITHMS

Sorting algorithms are used to arrange data within a list into a defined order.

BUBBLE SORT

A bubble sort is a simple sorting algorithm. It involves the following steps.

One pass

1 Compare the first two items in the list. If they are in order, leave them as they are. If items are not in order, swap them. In this example 4 is larger than 2 so they need to be swapped.

2 Repeat step 1 for items 2 and 3 in the list. In this example 4 is smaller than 7 so they do not need to be swapped.

3 Continue applying step 1 to the rest of the items in the list.

Once one pass is completed, repeat the process again and again until no swaps are required and all the numbers are in order.

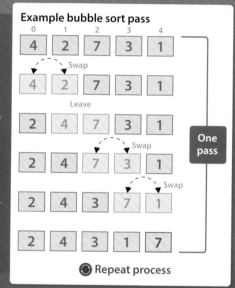

Example bubble sort pass

One pass

◉ Repeat process

An algorithm for a bubble sort on a list could look like this:

```
BEGIN BubbleSort(list)
  FOR i = 0 to (lengthOfList - 1)
    IF list[i] > list[i + 1] THEN
      swap(list[i], list[i + 1])
    ENDIF
    i = i + 1
  ENDFOR

  RETURN list
END BubbleSort
```

A bubble sort is likely to require multiple passes through the array, so it can be inefficient and unsuitable for large lists.

daydream EDUCATION

INSERTION SORT

An insertion sort is a simple sorting algorithm. It involves the following steps.

1 An insertion sort is a simple sorting algorithm that places each item, one at a time, into its correct place in a list.

2 The first item in the list is used as the starting point.

3 Each item in the list is compared to the items before it to determine where it needs to be placed.

An algorithm for an insertion sort on a list could look like this.

```
FOR i = 0 to (lengthOfList - 1)
  var j = i
  WHILE j > 0 AND list[j-1] > list[j]
    swap(list[j], list[j - 1])
    j = j - 1
  ENDWHILE
  i = i + 1
ENDFOR
```

Like a bubble sort, an insertion sort is easily coded and good for small lists, but it isn't an efficient sorting method for long lists.

Example insertion sort pass

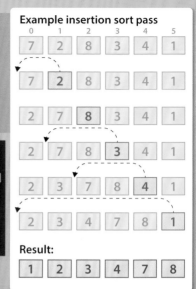

Result:

1	2	3	4	7	8

MERGE SORT

A merge sort is a 'divide and conquer' algorithm that splits a list into discrete elements and then merges the elements together in order.

1 Split the list in half to create two subsets.

2 Continue to split the subsets in half, until only individual items remain.

3 Merge individual items together in pairs, putting them back together in order.

4 Continue to merge the pairs together, with each subset being sorted in order.

5 Once all subsets have been combined, the list should be in order.

Example merge sort pass

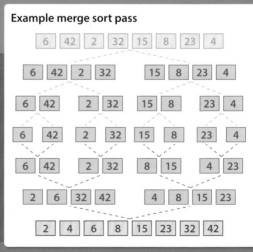

A merge sort is quicker and more efficient than a bubble sort or insertion sort when using longer lists. However, it uses more memory and can take longer to sort shorter lists.

SEARCHING ALGORITHMS

Searching algorithms are used to locate and retrieve information within a collection of data.

LINEAR SEARCH

A linear search looks at each item in a list sequentially (one item at a time) until the desired search item is located or until all the items have been searched.

Linear searches are relatively simple, but they are inefficient when searching through long lists.

Example — Find the search item **31**

Search item found.

BINARY SEARCH

A binary search is a much more efficient way of searching for items in a long list (dataset). However, for a binary search to work, the dataset must be ordered.

A binary search quickly reduces the size of the dataset by successively dividing it into two subsets until the search item is located.

1 Find the midpoint of the dataset:

Midpoint = (First + Last) ÷ 2
= (0 + 7) ÷ 2
= 3.5 ← round up to 4

2 If the search item is the midpoint value then the search item has been found.

31 > 27 so the search item has not been found.

3 If the search item is more than the midpoint value, discard the lower half of data and search for the item in the upper half of the data.

31 > 27 so discard the lower half of the data.

4 If the search item is less than the midpoint value, discard the upper half of data and search for the item in the lower half of the data.

31 < 42 so discard the upper half of the data.

5 Repeat steps 1–4 until the search item is located.

Midpoint value = 31 so search item has been found.

Example — Find the search item **31**

First point = 0   Midpoint = 4 / Midpoint value = 27   Last point = 7

Search item > Midpoint value. Discard lower half of list.

Search item < Midpoint value. Discard upper half of list.

Midpoint value = search item. Search item found.

daydream
EDUCATION

DATA TYPES

Data can consist of numbers, characters, symbols or images. Data can be stored in many different forms called 'data types'. These forms determine what actions can be performed on the data when it is assigned to a variable in programming, or a field in a database or spreadsheet.

INTEGER

Integers are whole numbers that can be either positive or negative. Examples of integers include: −10, −2, 6, 736, 16328 and 32415.

Integers are usually subcategorised in accordance with their ability to contain negative values. For example, within the C++ programming language, the unsigned short data type deals with numbers from 0 to 65535. In contrast, the short data type deals with numbers from −32768 to +32767.

Each programming language deals with integers in a different way.

REAL

Real data types contain numeric data in a decimal form. Real data types are useful in instances where more accurate information is required. For example, real data types may be used to represent distance in kilometres (e.g. 5.62 km) or weight in kilograms (e.g. 3.6 kg).

However, a real data type cannot store the unit of measure (e.g. kilometres) or its abbreviation (e.g. km).

STRING

A **string** is a list of characters that can contain text, numbers, symbols or punctuation. A string can be a combination of any of these items and often vary in length.

Names
Addresses
Telephone numbers
Car registrations

When string data types are used to store numbers, you cannot perform any sort of calculations on them.

CHARACTER

Character data types contain a single character from a character set, such as ASCII or Unicode. Each character has its own binary pattern.

Char	Binary
A	01000001
a	01100001
j	01101010
M	01001101

BOOLEAN

The **Boolean data type** is used to represent one of two values, true or false. Boolean logic is used in programming to return a true or false action or a 1 for true and a 0 for false. This makes it easy to control the flow of a program.

Logical Operators

AND is used when both data items need to be true for the computer to take action.

OR is used when only one item needs to be true for the computer to take action.

NOT is used when both data items need to be false for the computer to take action.

1. IF sky is blue AND sun is shining THEN show "summer"
2. Boolean logic evaluates each expression to see if it is either true or false.
3. IF (true) AND (true) THEN show "summer"
4. If either statement were false, then no action would be taken.
5. Most programming languages can understand Boolean logic when
6. parentheses are added:
7. IF (sky is blue) AND (sun is shining) THEN show "summer"

CASTING

Casting is used to transfer one data type into another data type. For example, the code int(x) would convert x to an integer. Other casting commands include float(), str() and bool ().

```
1
2  x = '30'
3  y = '-10'
4  Print(x + y)
5
```
This code would print 30 −10 because the numbers are strings, which cannot be used in calculations.

```
1
2  x = '30'
3  y = '-10'
4  Print(int(x) + int(y))
5
```
This code would print 20 as x and y are recognised as integers, which can be used in calculations.

daydream
EDUCATION

CONSTANTS AND VARIABLES

Data values can be stored as constants or variables. Constants remain the same and cannot be altered, whereas variables can be altered.

WHAT IS A CONSTANT?

In computer programming, a constant is a data item with values that cannot be changed by the program during normal execution.

Examples:

| PI = 3.14159 | → | Mathematical constants, like π, never change, so they can be assigned a specific (constant) value. |

| CONFIG = "config.json" | → | Many programs need to call a configuration file every time they run. Therefore, the configuration file can be assigned a specific CONFIG (constant) value. |

| TIMER = 90 | → | Something that must be kept constant to be fair, like the allotted time for a test, can be assigned a specific TIMER (constant) value. |

NAMING CONSTANTS

The value of a constant is given a name, also known as an identifier. The identifier is inserted into the code whenever the value is required.

You can use almost any name for a constant. A very common approach when naming constants is to use CAPITAL LETTERS. This makes it easier to see where a constant is used in the code rather than a variable. For example:

```
1
2      In this case, the constant 'DAYDREAM_WEBSITE' stands
       out as it is in capital letters and will never change
3      when the code is run.
4
5  const DAYDREAM_WEBSITE = "www.daydreameducation.co.uk"
6  var my_message = "Hello"
7
8  print(my_message, DAYDREAM_WEBSITE)
```

Hello
www.daydreameducation.co.uk

Identifiers are defined at the start of the code, and can then be used throughout the program by the programmer to make coding easier.

If the value of a constant needs to be changed, it must be done at the beginning of the code, where the constant is defined.

daydream
EDUCATION

WHAT IS A VARIABLE?

In computer programming, a variable is a data item with values that can be changed by the program during normal execution.

Examples:

Local

Declared inside a function (subprogram), and can only be accessed inside that function.

Main Program

Subprogram

Global

Declared outside any function (subprogram), usually at the start of the main program. They can be accessed throughout the whole program.

Main Program

Subprogram

NAMING VARIABLES

Every variable has a unique name, or identifier. This identifier refers to the location of the data within the memory.

Variables often start with a letter of the alphabet, contain an underscore and are written in sentence case. After the first initial letter, variable names may contain other letters and the digits 0 to 9. For example:

```
1  const DAYDREAM_WEBSITE = "www.daydreameducation.co.uk"
2  var my_message = "Good Afternoon"
3
4  print(my_message, DAYDREAM_WEBSITE)
5
6
7
8
```

Good Afternoon
www.daydreameducation.co.uk

In this case, the variable is 'my_message', and its contents can change every time the code is run.

Each programming language has its own set of restricted words that are reserved for its own use, and cannot be used as an identifier.

For example, some of the restricted words in Java include: 'abstract', 'Boolean', 'byte' and 'import'.

Variable	An identifier that points to a value that can change.
Constant	An identifier that points to a value that doesn't change.
Value	A number, string or character.

PROGRAM FLOW CONTROL

SEQUENCE

A sequence is a series of instructions in which each instruction is processed after the previous one has been executed.

Flow chart:

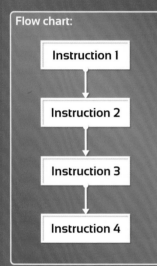

Code example:

```
Get first result
Get second result
Total = first result +
second result
Display "Overall result
is" + Total
```

FLOW CONTROL STRUCTURES

NO ◀ Is there an instruction that depends on a condition being true or false?

YES

NO ◀ Do the instructions need to be repeated until the desired answer is achieved?

YES

ITERATION

SELECTION

A selection is required when an instruction depends on a condition being true or false in order to be processed.

Flow chart:

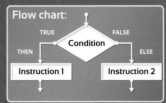

Code example:

There are two basic selection constructs: IF...THEN...ELSE and the CASE statement.

1. IF...THEN...ELSE provides a choice between two options.

This statement will be executed if the IF...THEN condition is true.

```
IF (x > 5) THEN
    Display (x)
ELSE
    x = x + 1
END IF
```

The **END IF** statement indicates that the condition has ended.

The statement after **ELSE** will be executed if the condition is false.

2. A CASE statement is more efficient when there are more than two options, such as when there is a menu with multiple options.

```
CASE MenuChoice OF
    A: Display (A)
    B: Display (B)
    C: Display (C)
    D: Display (D)
ELSE
    Display "You must
    select an option."
END CASE
```

This would require four separate IF...THEN...ELSE statements. The computer would then have to execute all four IF statements even when the user selects one menu option.

daydream
EDUCATION

Program flow control is the order in which a program is executed. Programmers can control the order of execution by using control structures. A control structure is a block of code that contains instructions and statements that determine the order of other instructions and statements. Programmers use flow charts to represent flow control structures. There are three different flow control structures that every programming language supports: sequence, selection and iteration.

ITERATION

An iteration is required when a series of instructions need to be repeated until the desired answer is achieved. A set of instructions that is repeatedly executed is known as a loop. The loop (in the diagram below) will continue to repeat until a false statement is reached.

Flow chart:

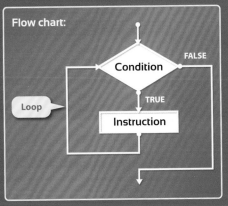

Code example:

There are three basic iteration constructs: the FOR loop, the REPEAT loop and the WHILE loop.

1. A FOR loop enables a set of instructions to be repeated a fixed number of times.

```
FOR count = 1 to 10 DO
     Display (count)
NEXT count
```

The start value is 1 and the end value is 10. Once the count has reached 10, the loop will terminate.

2. In a REPEAT loop, the number of repetitions is determined by a condition at the end of the loop.
Because the condition is checked at the end of the loop, a REPEAT loop always executes at least once.

```
count = 1
REPEAT
     Display (count)
     count = count + 1
UNTIL count = 20
```

Once the count has reached 20, the loop will terminate.

3. In a WHILE loop, the number of repetitions is determined by a condition at the start of the loop. Depending on the condition, a WHILE loop may not execute at all.

```
count = 1
WHILE count < 10 DO
     Display (count)
     count = count + 1
END WHILE
```

The loop will only execute when the count is less than 10.

ADVANTAGES OF USING CONTROL STRUCTURES

Control structures clarify the order of execution in a clear manner.	Using small sections of code allows several programmers to work on a program at the same time, increasing productivity.	The structures help programmers to find errors before the program is executed.	By breaking large amounts of code into smaller sections, programmers can update programs by easily editing individual sections of text.	Control structures break code into small, manageable sections.

PROGRAM FLOW EXAMPLE

```
Code Editor

    main.file

1   /*
2     Below is a pseudocode example of a
3     password routine that demonstrates
4     methods of program flow.
5   */
6
7   var password string
8   var username string
9   var userPassword string
10
11  password = "MANAGER286"
12  username = input("What is your username?")
13  username = username.toLower()
14
15  print("Hi " + username + " how are you today?")
16
17  SUBPROGRAM passwordCheck BEGIN
18    userPassword = input("Please enter your password")
19
20    IF userPassword == password THEN
21      print("Welcome to the system manager")
22    ELSE
23      print("Login details incorrect")
24      passwordCheck()
25    ENDIF
26
27  ENDSUBPROGRAM
28
```

Variables are declared for use in the program.

password set to "MANAGER286".

Ask for a username, store it in a variable called username and convert it to lower case.

Print message using username stored in the username variable.

Start of passwordCheck subprogram.

Ask user to enter password and store it in a variable called userPassword.

If the contents of the userPassword and password ("MANAGER286") are equal, the program displays a welcome message.

If the contents of the userPassword and password ("MANAGER286") are not equal, the program displays an error message.

The passwordCheck() command directs the program back to the start of the passwordCheck subprogram.

daydream
EDUCATION

DATA STRUCTURES

A data structure is a collection of related data items that are stored together in a clear, structured form. A data structure provides an efficient method for managing large amounts of data and organising data to make it suitable for computer processing. There are different types of data structures, including arrays and linked lists, which are used in different situations.

ARRAYS

An array is a collection of data items of the same data type that are stored under a single identifier (name). The items within the array are called the array elements; they can be accessed by referencing their position within the array.

One-Dimensional Arrays

One-dimensional arrays are data structures that allow lists of items to be stored. The items are then accessed by detailing their position within the array. The arrays are one-dimensional because a single number is used to refer to each element's position in the array.

An example of an array in PHP code:

```php
<?php
    $sportsTeams = array[Football, Rugby, Hockey];
?>
```

The variable 'sportsTeams' is defined as an array. To access an item in the array, the item's position number is used. This is called indexing.

For example to access 'Hockey' in the example array:

```php
<?php
    $sport_name = sportsTeams [2] ;
?>
```

In programming, [0] refers to the first position, [1] refers to the second position, [2] refers to the third position and so on.

Two-Dimensional Arrays

Two-dimensional arrays store and access information within a matrix or grid made up of rows and columns. Each row contains an array, also known as a sub-array.

For example:

	0	1	2	3
0	1	2	3	4
1	5	6	7	8
2	9	10	11	12
3	13	14	15	16
4	17	18	19	20
5	21	22	23	24

This array is named **numbers**. It has **6** rows and **4** columns, indicating that there are 6 sub-arrays within the main array and 4 elements in each sub-array.

To define it as a data structure, in code it is written as:

```
$numbers [6] [4];
```

LINKED LISTS

A linked list is a group of items, each of which contains the data and a pointer that points to the next item. This enables the items to be accessed in order even if they are not stored in order.

A linked list allocates an area of memory, known as a linked list element or node, for each individual item. The list achieves its overall structure by using pointers to connect all of its nodes together. Linked lists can appear as singly linked lists or doubly linked lists.

A singly linked list is created in one direction, so the pointers have only one arrow that points to the next element.

> A terminator is used to signify the end of a list.

A doubly linked list is created in two directions, so the pointers have two arrows that point to both the next element in the sequence and the previous element.

BINARY TREES

A **binary tree** is a hierarchical data structure that is often used in directories of files. In a binary tree, data items, known as nodes, appear at different levels and are linked by branches.

Any node with a node below it is known as a parent node. Each parent node is linked to a maximum of two child nodes that hold data related to the parent node.

The topmost node is called the root node. It is the only node in a tree without a parent node.

Nodes without children are referred to as leaf nodes. A leaf node indicates the end of a tree structure at a given point.

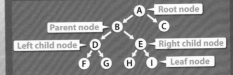

A binary search tree is a particular type of binary tree that is useful for storing data that requires rapid access, storage and deletion.

daydream
EDUCATION

QUERY METHODS

A query is a question used to extract information from a database. The computer checks each record of data to see if it satisfies the query. Each record answers the query with either true or false. A report is produced that includes a list of all the data that satisfies the query.

Structured Query Language (SQL) was developed as a method of setting up databases and performing tasks on the data. SQL commands are used for storing, retrieving and manipulating data in a relational database. Below are some examples of the most commonly used SQL commands.

CREATING A DATABASE

The following command is used to set up a database called 'daydream':

CREATE DATABASE daydream

DELETING DATA

To delete data from the table, the **DELETE FROM** command is used.

SQL command | Table name

```
DELETE FROM customers
WHERE customer_id = 0003;
```

The **WHERE** clause specifies which records should be deleted.

The above code would delete John Rogers from the table.

SORTING DATA

To sort the data in a database, the **ORDER BY** statement is used.

```
SELECT * FROM customers
 ORDER BY last_name DESC
;
```

This will sort the data by last name in descending (DESC) order from Z to A. To sort the data in ascending order from A to Z, ASC would be used instead of DESC.

CREATING A TABLE

A database consists of one or more tables. Tables are made up of columns and rows. Columns contain a column name and store a specific data type. Rows contain the records or data for each column. A table is given a name that it can be identified by in the commands. To create a table, the SQL command **CREATE TABLE** is used.

first_name	last_name	email_address	customer_id
Charlie	Walker	charlie@example.com	0001
Laura	Jones	laura@example.com	0002
John	Rogers		0003

To produce the table above called customers, the code would be written as follows:

SQL command | Table name

```
CREATE TABLE customers (
    first_name CHAR (20) NULL,
    last_name CHAR (30) NULL,
    email_address VARCHAR (50) NULL,
    customer_id INT IDENTITY (0001, 1) NOT NULL,
) ;
```

CHAR represents a character column. The number that follows indicates the character limit. Thus, CHAR (20) can store up to 20 characters.

NULL means this column can be empty if the details are not available.

VARCHAR represents a column that can store a combination of letters and numbers.

INT represents a column that stores integers.

(0001, 1) states that the column should start with 0001 and increase by 1 in each subsequent row.

NOT NULL means that this column cannot be empty because it is required for the database to work.

54

daydream
EDUCATION

THE SQL SELECT STATEMENT

The **SELECT** command is used to extract records from a database. To extract **all** records from the table, the following code is used:

SQL command — The **FROM** statement is followed by the table name.

```
SELECT * FROM customers
```

The * symbol means all fields.

To extract a **particular set** of records from the data, the **WHERE** clause is needed:

After the **SELECT** clause, outline the fields from which data will be extracted.

```
SELECT last_name, email_address
    FROM customers
    WHERE last_name = 'Jones' ;
```

The **WHERE** clause specifies which records are to be extracted.

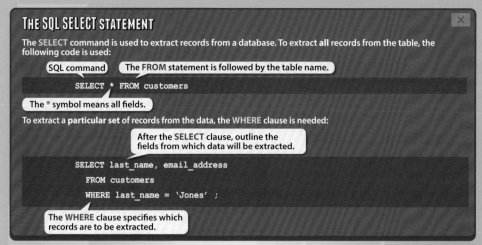

THE SQL INSERT INTO STATEMENT

To add records into a table, the **INSERT INTO** command is used.

SQL command   Table name

```
INSERT INTO customers (first_name,
    last_name,
    email_address)
VALUES ('John',
    'Rogers',
    NULL) ;
```

Within the brackets, include the names of the fields to which new data will be uploaded.

The SQL term **VALUES** appears before the data values to be inserted.

If data for a particular field is not available, enter **NULL** into the code.

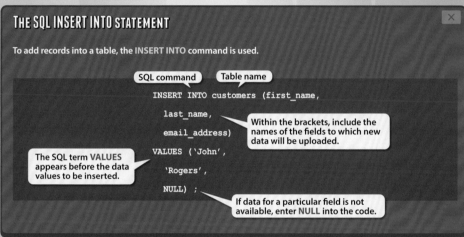

THE SQL UPDATE STATEMENT

To edit existing records in a table, the **UPDATE** statement is used.

SQL command   Table name

```
UPDATE customers
    SET email_address =
    'charlie123@example.co.uk'
WHERE customer_id = 0001;
```

Enter the updated version of the data to be included in the field.

The **SET** command should be followed by the field which is to be updated.

The **WHERE** clause outlines which record is to be updated.

The above code would change Charlie Walker's email address.

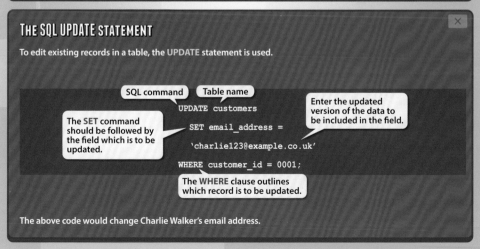

PROCEDURES AND FUNCTIONS

Procedures and functions are subprograms that break down large programs into smaller, more manageable sections. They are used in all programming languages.

WHAT ARE SUBPROGRAMS?

Programs consist of modules of code that perform different tasks. If these tasks are repeated throughout the program, they can be written as subprograms.

Each subprogram is given a unique name so that it can be called and executed quickly throughout the program, without having to write the code again. This reduces the size of code, making the program more logical and easier to read and maintain.

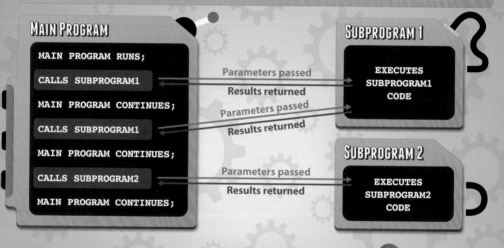

MAIN PROGRAM

```
MAIN PROGRAM RUNS;

CALLS SUBPROGRAM1

MAIN PROGRAM CONTINUES;

CALLS SUBPROGRAM1

MAIN PROGRAM CONTINUES;

CALLS SUBPROGRAM2

MAIN PROGRAM CONTINUES;
```

Parameters passed
Results returned
Parameters passed
Results returned

SUBPROGRAM 1

```
EXECUTES
SUBPROGRAM1
CODE
```

Parameters passed
Results returned

SUBPROGRAM 2

```
EXECUTES
SUBPROGRAM2
CODE
```

PARAMETERS

Parameters allow values to be passed to procedures and functions for their use. For the following function, the value of x must be provided.

Input

```
FUNCTION Square: x integer;
BEGIN
   var result = x * x;
   return result;
END;
```

2 × 2

When the function is called within the main program, the value of x is defined within the parameters. Parameters are always defined in brackets.

```
BEGIN
   Write_line(Square(2));
END;
```

The values are then sent to be used by the function. This function returns the value resulting from squaring 2, which is 4.

Output

Variables are data items with values that can be changed after a program has been compiled.

Local variables are only available within the subprogram.

Global variables are available throughout the whole program.

daydream
EDUCATION

Subprograms can fall into two categories:
procedures and functions.

Type: Procedures ▼

A procedure receives data from a program and performs a specified action on the data. It will not return a value to the program, but it will make the results available. Procedures are used to reduce the size of a program and avoid repetitions in code. By breaking code down into smaller sections, procedures make code easier to read and debug.

How to use a procedure

1. To create a procedure, first define it and give it a name. The following example is used to create a procedure that displays the greeting 'Hello Everyone!' three times on the computer screen.

Name of the procedure

var tells the computer that a variable is about to be declared.

```
PROCEDURE greeting;
   var n integer;
BEGIN
   FOR n := 1 to 3
      Write_line('Hello Everyone!');
   ENDFOR
END;
```

Contents of the procedure

2. To execute a procedure, use a procedure call statement. The procedure call statement refers to the name of the procedure as shown in the example below.

```
BEGIN
   greeting();
END;
```

The above call would print the below:

```
Hello Everyone! Hello
Everyone! Hello Everyone!
```

3. Once a procedure has been executed, the program returns to the place in the code immediately after where the procedure was called.

Type: Functions ▼

A function computes a value using data provided by the program and returns a single value to the program. It is similar to a procedure, but a procedure cannot return a value.

How to use a function

1. Before a function can be executed, it must be defined and given a name. The following example is used to create a function that multiplies the value of a by the value of b.

Name of the function   Parameters passed in

```
FUNCTION Multiply: a, b integer;
BEGIN
   var result = a * b;
   return result;
END;
```

Declaring the data type

Contents of the function

2. A function subprogram can be executed anywhere within a program if it is called. Along with the call, parameters (in this case, the numbers to multiply) can be passed to the subprogram (see below).

```
BEGIN
   Write_line(Multiply(4, 2));
END;
```

3. This function will return the value resulting from multiplying 4 by 2, which is 8. Once the function has been executed, the program returns to the place in the code immediately after where the function was called.

Built-in functions are provided by the particular programming language that is being used. They are already coded and available for the programmer to call from within the main program. They are very useful and save the programmer time and effort in writing code for certain tasks.

PROGRAMMING OPERATORS

MATHEMATICAL OPERATORS
Perform mathematical functions on integer and real data values

Operator	Meaning	Example
+	Addition	4 + 4 = 8
−	Subtraction	4 − 4 = 0
*	Multiplication	4 * 4 = 16
/	Division	12 / 4 = 3
^	Exponentiation	4^2 = 16
&	String concatenation	"4" & "4" = "44"
MOD or %	Modulus (returns the remainder value after division)	11MOD3 = 2
DIV	Quotient (returns the whole number value after division)	11DIV3 = 3

The acronym BIDMAS is used to remember the correct order of operation:
Brackets, Indices, Division or Multiplication, Addition or Subtraction

ASSIGNMENT OPERATORS
Assign a value to a variable, property, event or indexer

The equals sign, =, is an assignment operator that is used to assign values to constants and variables. The assigned value is always to the right of the equals sign.

```
radius = 5        name = "Craig"        pi = 3.14159        y = 23
```

COMPARISON OPERATORS
Compare expressions to produce a Boolean value (true or false)

Operator	Meaning	Example		
		Variables	Condition	Result
==	Is equal to (values only)	a = 3, b = 7	a == b	FALSE
!=	Is not equal to	x = 2, y = 4	x != y	TRUE
>	Is greater than	c = 4, d = 1	c > d	TRUE
<	Is less than	a = 9, b = 21	b < a	FALSE
>=	Is greater than or equal to	x = 5, y = 3	x >= y	TRUE
<=	Is less than or equal to	c = 4, d = 4	c <= d	TRUE

BOOLEAN OPERATORS
Can connect or reverse conditions

Operator	Meaning	Example		
		Variables	Condition	Result
AND	Multiple conditions must be met	w = 2, x = 4, y = 3, z = 1	(w > z) AND (x > y)	TRUE
OR	Only one condition needs to be met	a = 3, b = 9, c = 6, d = 4	(a == d) OR (c >= d)	TRUE
NOT	Reverses a condition	n = 8, m = 5	NOT (n > m)	FALSE

daydream
EDUCATION

Basic HTML

Web pages are written in a Hypertext Mark-up Language (HTML). HTML is mainly used to define the structure of a web page's content whilst Cascading Style Sheets (CSS) are used to define how the content is styled. HTML code can be written in a basic text editor and saved as an HTML file. The file can then be run in a web browser and displayed as a web page.

Example of a basic web page written in HTML:

```html
<html>
<head>
<title>About Me Page</title>
</head>
<body>
        <h1>Amy Smith</h1>
        <h2>Interesting Facts About Me</h2>
        <p>I study computer science.</p>
        <img src="pictures/me.jpg">
</body>
</html>
```

About Me Page

Amy Smith
Interesting Facts About Me
I study computer science.

Tags

HTML code uses tags to define a web page's structure and characterise parts of the text. Tags are generally used in pairs consisting of a start tag and an end tag to separate sections of text. A tag includes the name of the relevant text element enclosed in a pair of angle brackets (e.g. <html>). Tag names reflect their function. End tags include a forward slash to indicate a section's end (e.g. </html>).

Name	Tag	What does it do?
HTML tag	<html> </html>	This tag indicates that you will be coding the web page in HTML.
Head tag	<head> </head>	Head tags surround title tags and provide the structure for the placement of the title. This tag can include information such as font, styles and metadata.
Title tag	<title> </title>	This tag defines the title that appears in the browser toolbar and in search-engine results. The title tags are placed between the head tags.
Body tag	<body> </body>	After the head section, you must outline what is going to be included in the main section of the web page, known as the body.
Paragraph tag	<p> </p>	These tags are used to start a new paragraph. Unlike in emails or word processing software, pressing Enter will not create a new paragraph.
Heading tag	<h1> </h1> <h6> </h6>	This tag indicates the heading level and, thus, the heading size, with 1 being the first and largest heading and 6 being the last and smallest heading.
Break tag	 	This tag is used to create a line break, or to move text to a new line.
Image source tag	<img src="pictures/me.jpg">	This tag references a picture file and the folder where it is saved.
Bold tag	<b> </b>	This tag is used to make the text between the tags bold.
Underline tag	<u> </u>	This tag is used to underline the text between the tags.
Italics tag	<i> </i>	This tag is used to italicise the text between the tags.
Font colour tag*	<font color= "blue"> </font color>	This tag is used to change font colour. Note that HTML uses American spelling, so the code is spelt color.
Font size tag*	<font size ="7"> </font>	This tag changes the text size within a web page's main body. The number represents the font size, with 1 being the smallest and 7 being the largest.

*These tags are no longer supported in HTML5

Publishing Web Pages to the Internet

You can view an HTML web page you have created in a web browser because you can access the file on your computer. For other people to access the page online, it must be uploaded onto a web server so it can be published to the Internet.

Hosting services can provide server space to people who do not have their own server. Coding a website in HTML can be time-consuming, but there are many available software applications that can simplify the coding process.

59

DEFENSIVE DESIGN

During the design of a program, it is important to consider any potential problems, and put a plan in place to prevent them from occurring. This will involve anticipating how users may misuse the program and ensuring that code is well-maintained and error free.

INPUT VALIDATION AND SANITISATION

Input validation and sanitisation are used to ensure that no erroneous data is entered into a program. These two techniques are often used together.

Input Validation

Input validation checks whether the input data meets a set of criteria. For example, if the data is of the correct type, range, format and length.

```
1  SUBPROGRAM isValidLength: value;
2  BEGIN
3    var requiredLength = 11
4    var length = value.length()
5    IF length == requiredLength
6      return true
7    ELSE
8      return false
9    ENDIF
10 ENDSUBPROGRAM
```

The above is an example of a validation check for a mobile phone number input field. It checks that the character length is equal to eleven characters; the standard length for a UK mobile phone number.

Input Sanitisation

Input sanitisation modifies input data to ensure that it is valid. This is extremely useful to help protect against web attacks where code injection is used.

```
1  SUBPROGRAM escapeHtml: str;
2    str.replace(/&/g, '&amp;')
3    str.replace(/</g, '&lt;')
4    str.replace(/>/g, '&gt;')
5    str.replace(/"/g, '&quot;')
6    str.replace(/'/g, '&#x27;')
7    str.replace(/\//g, '&#x2F;')
8    return str;
9  ENDSUBPROGRAM
```

The above is an example of a sanitisation check for preventing the injection of client-side scripts into web pages. Characters that are often used to execute harmful code have been replaced with HTML entity encoding.

Input validation and sanitisation ensure that the entered data follows the rules set out in the code. However, it does not necessarily mean that the data is accurate.

AUTHENTICATION

Authentication is used to prevent unauthorised access to a program and to set levels of access for authorised users.

Usernames and passwords are often used to confirm the identity of users and ensure they have the correct level of access to the program or part of the program.

Password-based authentication, such as minimum character length, is also used to ensure that passwords are difficult to guess.

MAINTENANCE

Programs need to be well structured so that they are easy to maintain. A well-structured program will:

- Use indents to help programmers identify the program flow and structure

- Have clearly named variables and subprograms that reflect their purpose

- Include comments that explain the main features of the program

daydream
EDUCATION

TESTING

When developing a program, tests should be performed throughout the process to ensure that the program functions correctly, is error free and meets the specification requirements.

Error Handling

Tests should be completed to identify any coding errors or bugs. There are three types of errors that commonly occur when computer programmers write code:

❌ Syntax Errors

What are they? Syntax is a set of rules that state how a program's code must be formatted. Syntax errors happen when a computer programmer does not obey the grammar rules of the programming language being used.

Common causes: The wrong letter case is used. Punctuation is inserted in the wrong place. Reserved words or variables are spelt incorrectly.

❌ Run-time Errors

What are they? Run-time errors happen when a program instructs a computer to carry out a task that it either cannot do or is slow to perform. Run-time errors occur during a program's execution.

Common causes: There is insufficient memory available on the computer. Unusual data is encountered. A program instructs a computer to divide a number by zero.

❌ Logic Errors

What are they? Logic errors are mistakes in the design of a program that cause the program to behave in an unexpected way. Logic errors will not stop a program from running, but they will produce incorrect results.

Common causes: The programmer has not understood the purpose of the program. The programmer has not understood the individual behaviour of each operation that is part of the program.

Translators, such as compilers, will identify syntax errors in the code. These must be fixed before the program can run. It is also vital to perform other tests, such as functional tests, to identify logic and run-time errors and ensure that the program performs correctly.

Functional Testing

Tests should be completed to ensure that the program performs all the functionality stated within the initial specification requirements. Performance, security, usability and fault tolerance should also be tested.

Iterative Testing

Iterative testing involves testing a program at every stage of the development cycle. Individual parts of the program are tested to ensure that they function correctly.

As parts are combined, the program can then be tested to see if any errors have been introduced, or if there are any conflicts between the different parts.

Final Testing

Final testing is the last phase of testing that checks that all the specification requirements of the project have been met. Various input data is fed into the program to test that it performs as expected.

1 → 2 → 3 → 4

Selecting Suitable Test Data

It is important to select suitable input data when testing a program. Test data should include:

Normal data: data that should be accepted by the program and is typical of what a user is likely to input into the program.	**Extreme data:** data that should be accepted by the program but is at the limits of the acceptable input range.	**Erroneous data:** data that is invalid and should be rejected.

Using a wide range of test data will ensure the program is robust and able to cope with a variety of conditions and values.

TRANSLATORS

HIGH-LEVEL AND LOW-LEVEL LANGUAGES

Low-level Languages

Low-level languages are used for tasks that are associated with the running of a computer. They provide instructions on how a computer will execute a program based on how the machine is built. Therefore, they generally do not work on any other type of machine. Low-level languages are complex and difficult to read, but computers can execute them quickly and efficiently.

| High-level Languages |
| Assembly Language |
| Machine Code |
| Hardware |

High-level Languages

Programmers find it easier to read and write programs in high-level language: code that looks more like normal languages. The code details how a problem is to be solved rather than giving instructions on how the computer will provide a solution. High-level languages can be used on a variety of different machines. However, they are not as efficient as low-level languages.

TRANSLATORS

High-level language and assembly language needs to be translated in to machine code for a computer system to understand it. This translation is performed by translators.

Assemblers

Assembly language uses command words called 'mnemonics', such as LOAD, STORE and ADD. The instructions are specific to the hardware being programmed because different CPUs use different programming languages.

Assemblers are used to convert assembly language into machine code.

Assembly Code → Assembler → Machine Code

Compilers and Interpreters

A set of instructions written in a high-level language is known as source code. The source code is translated into machine code that a computer can run using compilers or interpreters.

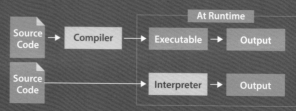

Compilers translate all the source code at the same time to create the compiled code, or executable file. Compiling can take a long time, but once complete, the compiled code runs quickly and reports a list of errors, if any have occurred.

Interpreters translate source code into machine code one command at a time and immediately execute it. If an error is found, the interpreter stops so it can be debugged and corrected straight away.

Interpreters do not create an executable file, so they must translate the code every time the program is run. The code also runs slower than compiled code because it is being translated and executed one command at a time.

daydream
EDUCATION

INTEGRATED DEVELOPMENT ENVIRONMENTS

An integrated development environment (IDE), or software development environment (SDE), provides programmers with tools to create computer programs. Here are some of the tools and facilities offered by IDEs.

IDE FEATURES

Runtime Environment

The runtime environment (RTE) allows programmers to test a program while it is running. Programmers can track the instructions being processed by the program and debug any errors that may arise. If the program crashes, the RTE software keeps running and may provide important information about why the program crashed.

Daydream IDE   ○ ○ ○

File   Edit   View   ▶ Start

Editor - code/fib.py	Output Window	Explorer Window

```python
# Python: Fibonacci series up to 10 numbers
numbers = 10
a, b = 0, 1

print a
print b

for d in range(numbers - 2):
    c = a + b
    print c
    a, b = b, c
```

Output Window:
```
0
1
1
2
3
5
8
13
21
34
```

Explorer Window:
- code
  - fib.py

The editor allows a programmer to enter, format and edit source code. It is often optimised for a specific programming language.

The output window shows the result of a program once it has been run.

Using the explorer window, the programmer can navigate to different programs.

Breakpoint

A breakpoint interrupts a program on a specific line of code, allowing the programmer to compare the values of variables against expected values. It is helpful for debugging purposes.

Memory Inspector

A memory inspector displays the contents of a section of memory.

Error Diagnostics

Error diagnostics is used when a program fails to compile or to run. Error messages are displayed to help the programmer diagnose what has gone wrong.

Trace

A trace displays the order in which the lines of a program are executed and, possibly, the values of variables as the program is being run.

Translator

A facility for translating high-level language and assembly language into machine code so a computer system can understand it.

Object File 1
Object File 2
Object File 3

Linker

A computer program that takes one or more object files generated by a compiler and combines them into a single file.

Executable File

---

 daydream EDUCATION

LOGIC

Transistors on a computer chip are wired together to create logic gates that can perform simple logical calculations. Logic gates apply Boolean operations to one or more binary inputs to produce a single binary output.

LOGIC GATES AND TRUTH TABLES

Logic gates are often displayed using logic diagrams and truth tables. Truth tables show how the input(s) of a logic gate relate to its output.

NOT Gate

A NOT gate takes a single input and outputs the opposite value.

Logic Diagram

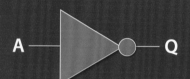

Truth Table

Input	Output
A	Q
1	0
0	1

AND Gate

An AND gate takes at least two inputs and identifies if all values are 1. If all inputs are 1, it outputs 1, otherwise 0 is output.

Logic Diagram

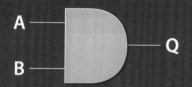

Truth Table

Input		Output
A	B	Q
0	0	0
1	0	0
0	1	0
1	1	1

OR Gate

An OR Gate takes at least two inputs and identifies if any of the values are 1. If at least one input is 1, it outputs 1, otherwise 0 is output.

Logic Diagram

Truth Table

Input		Output
A	B	Q
0	0	0
1	0	1
0	1	1
1	1	1

daydream
EDUCATION

REAL LIFE EXAMPLE

The example below shows a logic diagram and truth table for a simple alarm system.

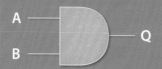

In order for the alarm to sound, both statements must be TRUE (1); ALARM must equal ON and DOOR must equal OPEN.

Inputs		Output
Alarm On (A)	Door Open (B)	Alarm Sounds (Q)
0	0	0
0	1	0
1	0	0
1	1	1

LOGIC CIRCUITS

Logic gates are often combined to create logic circuits that can perform more complex operations. In the example below, the AND and NOT gates have been combined.

EXPRESSION: R = NOT (A AND B)

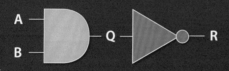

A	B	Q = A AND B	R = NOT Q
0	0	0	1
0	1	0	1
1	0	0	1
1	1	1	0

Some logic gates may have more than two inputs. For example, the diagram below shows a logic circuit that combines two logic gates and has three inputs.

EXPRESSION: R = (A OR B) AND C

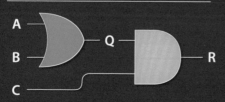

A and B are fed into an OR gate. Its output Q is then fed into an AND gate along with input C, to output R.

A	B	C	Q = A OR B	R = Q AND C
0	0	0	0	0
0	0	1	0	0
0	1	0	1	0
0	1	1	1	1
1	0	0	1	0
1	0	1	1	1
1	1	0	1	0
1	1	1	1	1

BINARY AND DENARY NUMBERS

WHY DO COMPUTERS USE BINARY NUMBERS?

Computers use binary numbers, the digits 0 and 1, to store data. This is because computer systems use switches to represent data and switches have only two states: ON and OFF.

ON corresponds to 1 and OFF corresponds to 0.

All computer programs, must therefore be translated into binary code for the computer to understand and execute the instructions.

Note: Humans cannot use this system easily.

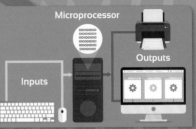

Microprocessor

Inputs

Outputs

BINARY NUMBERS

In computing, digital data is represented by **binary digits (bits)**. A bit can hold one of two values: 0 or 1. Bits are organised in groups of 8. A group of 8 bits is called a byte.

			8 bits = 1 byte				
0	1	1	0	1	0	1	1

1 nibble = 4 bits

Binary numbers are known as base 2 numbers because the binary system only uses two symbols, 0 and 1. Each bit in a byte represents a different power of 2:

×2　×2　×2　×2　×2　×2　×2

128	64	32	16	8	4	2	1
2^7	2^6	2^5	2^4	2^3	2^2	2^1	2^0

Bit values are often used to represent true/false, on/off and black/white.

CONVERTING BINARY TO DENARY

To convert a binary number into a denary number, add the numbers in the column headings for the columns that contain a 1. Look at the example below.

128	64	32	16	8	4	2	1	Total
1	0	1	0	1	1	0	0	128 + 32 + 8 + 4 = **172**

There is a 1 in the 128, 32, 8 and 4 columns, so add these together to find the denary number. Here are some more examples:

128	64	32	16	8	4	2	1	Total
0	0	0	0	0	1	0	1	4 + 1 = **5**
0	0	1	0	0	1	0	0	32 + 4 = **36**
1	1	1	0	0	1	1	0	128 + 64 + 32 + 4 + 2 = **230**

daydream
EDUCATION

DENARY NUMBERS

In a denary (base 10) number system, the digits 0-9 are used to represent powers of ten (1, 10, 100, 1,000 and so on).

345 =	Hundreds (100)	Tens (10)	Units (1)
	3	4	5
	(3×100)	(4×10)	(5×1)

CONVERTING DENARY TO BINARY

To convert a denary number into a binary number, follow the steps outlined below:

1. To convert **52** to a binary number, first find the biggest number in the **column headings** that is less than or equal to **52**. Place a **1** in the cell below that column heading.

> **32** is the biggest column heading that is less than **52**. **128** and **64** are too big.

Denary number	128	64	32	16	8	4	2	1
52			1					

> Place a **1** in this cell.

2. Subtract this column heading, **32**, from the **denary number**: **52 – 32 = 20**. Next, repeat step 1 with the answer, **20**:

> **16** is the biggest column heading that is less than or equal to **20**.

Denary number	128	64	32	16	8	4	2	1
52			1	1				

> Place a **1** in this cell.

3. Subtract this column heading, **16**, from the answer, **20**: **20 – 16 = 4**. Repeat step 1 with the answer, **4**, and then continue this process until you reach 0.

> **4** is the biggest column heading that is less than or equal to **4**.

Denary number	128	64	32	16	8	4	2	1
52			1	1		1		

> Place a **1** in this cell.

4. As **4 – 4 = 0**, the conversion is now complete. To check your answer, add the numbers in the column headings for the columns that contain a **1**. **52** represented as a binary number is **0011 0100**.

> **32 + 16 + 4 = 52**

Denary number	128	64	32	16	8	4	2	1
52	0	0	1	1	0	1	0	0

> Place a **0** in each empty cell.

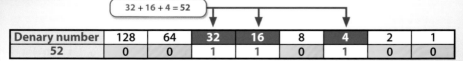

BINARY ADDITION

BINARY ADDITION

In the binary, or base 2, numeral system, there are only two digits, 0 and 1. This means that unlike in the denary numeral system 1 + 1 does not equal 2, it equals 10. Look at the binary addition examples to the right.

0 + 0 = 0	same as denary system
0 + 1 = 1	same as denary system
1 + 1 = 10	not the same as denary system

Binary addition can be performed using column addition. Because the largest value a one-digit binary number can have is 1, anything that exceeds this must be carried over to the next column (2) in the base-2 place value table.

	32	16	8	4	2	1
						1
+						1
Answer					1	0
Carried					1	

Look at how 0101 and 0111 have been added using column addition in the example below.

1. List the binary numbers underneath one another, so that the digits with the same place value are aligned vertically.

2. Starting at the column on the right-hand side, add the numbers in the same column.

3. If the total of one column is greater than 1, carry 1 over to the column to the left.

	8	4	2	1
	0	1	0	1
+	0	1	1	1
Answer	1	1	0	0
Carried	1	1	1	

1 + 1 = 10 and 10 + 1 = 11 so:
1 + 1 + 1 = 11

OVERFLOW ERRORS

An overflow error occurs when the answer to a binary addition equation is larger than the CPU is capable of handling.

For example, a CPU with a capacity of 8 bits can handle binary numbers up to 11111111. However, if one more bit was added to give 100000000, a 9-bit answer, the CPU would ignore the 1 and output 00000000, which is incorrect.

This results in an overflow error. There is a '1' in bit position 9, but only 8 bits can be used.

		8 bits							
		1	0	0	1	1	1	0	1
+		1	1	1	1	0	1	0	1
Answer	1	1	0	0	1	0	0	1	0
Carried	1	1	1	1	1	1		1	

daydream EDUCATION

BINARY SHIFTS

Background

In the binary, or base 2, numeral system, the value of a digit changes by a power of two when its place in a number shifts to the left or to the right.

Each digit to the left is double the value of the digit to its right.

×2	×2	×2	×2	×2	×2	×2
128	64	32	16	8	4	2	1
÷2	÷2	÷2	÷2	÷2	÷2	÷2

Each digit to the right is half the value of the digit to its left.

MULTIPLICATION

When a binary number is multiplied by a power of 2 there is a 'left shift' of bits.

| Binary | Denary |

Multiplying a binary number by 2^1 (2) shifts all digits one place to the left.

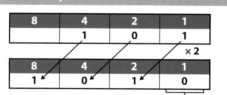

8	4	2	1
	1	0	1
			×2
8	4	2	1
1	0	1	0

When multiplying, fill each empty place to the right with a 0.

5
×2
10

A 3-place left shift, multiplies the number by 2^3 (8).

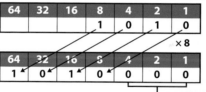

64	32	16	8	4	2	1
			1	0	1	0
						×8
64	32	16	8	4	2	1
1	0	1	0	0	0	0

When multiplying, fill each empty place to the right with a 0.

10
×8
80

DIVISION

When a binary number is divided by a power of 2 there is a 'right shift' of bits.

| Binary | Denary |

Dividing a binary number by 2^2 (4) shifts all digits two places to the right.

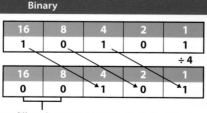

16	8	4	2	1
1	0	1	0	1
				÷4
16	8	4	2	1
0	0	1	0	1

When dividing, fill each empty place to the left with a 0.

20
÷4
5

HEXADECIMAL NUMBERS

Hexadecimal numbers (also hex, or base 16), use the digits 0–9 and the letters A–F, making 16 characters. So, a single hex digit can show 16 different values instead of 10, as in denary.

A single hex character is equal to 4 bits (a nibble) so in computing, short hex numbers are used to represent long binary patterns. This also makes it easier to convert between binary and hex than binary and denary.

 In the table below, hexadecimal numbers are shown with their denary and binary equivalents.

Denary	Binary	Hex
0	0000	0
1	0001	1
2	0010	2
3	0011	3
4	0100	4
5	0101	5
6	0110	6
7	0111	7
8	1000	8
9	1001	9
10	1010	A
11	1011	B
12	1100	C
13	1101	D
14	1110	E
15	1111	F

COUNTING IN HEXADECIMAL

When counting in denary, once a units, tens, hundreds or thousands column has reached 9, the column returns to 0, and 1 is added to the column to the left. As you move a column to the left, every number place is 10 times bigger than the one to the right.

When counting in hexadecimal, once a column has reached 9 it then moves onto the letters A–F. When F has been reached, the column returns to 0, and 1 is added to the column to the left. As you move a column to the left, every number place is 16 times bigger than the one to the right.

× 16	× 16	× 16	
4096	256	16	1
16^3	16^2	16^1	16^0

daydream EDUCATION

Converting Hex to Denary

To convert the hexadecimal number CB8 to denary:

1 Place the hexadecimal number into a base 16 place value table.

256	16	1
C	B	8

2 Identify what each hex digit represents in denary.

$C = 12$ $B = 11$ $8 = 8$

3 Multiply the answers by the column heading values.

$12 \times 256 = 3072$ $11 \times 16 = 176$ $8 \times 1 = 8$

4 Add the numbers together.

$3072 + 176 + 8 = 3256$

CB8 is equivalent to 3,256.

Converting Denary to Hex

To convert the denary number 164 to hex:

1 Divide the denary number by 16 and record the remainder.

$164 \div 16 = 10$ remainder 4

2 The remainder, 4, is the number of 1s, and the answer, 10, is the number of 16s.

10 in hex is A →

16	1
A	4

164 is equivalent to A4.

You can also convert denary to hex by converting denary to binary digits and then converting binary digits to hex.

Converting Binary to Hex

To convert 01001100 to hex:

1 Split 01001100 into nibbles, and place each nibble into a base 2 place value table.

0100   1100

8	4	2	1	8	4	2	1
0	1	0	0	1	1	0	0

2 For each nibble, add the column headings for the columns that contain a 1.

4                $8 + 4 = 12$

3 Convert the denary values to hex.

$4 = 4$ $12 = C$

01001100 is equivalent to 4C.

Converting Hex to Binary

To convert A6 to binary:

1 Convert each hex digit to binary.

A   6

8	4	2	1	8	4	2	1
1	0	1	0	0	1	1	0

$A = 10 = 8 + 2$ $6 = 4 + 2$

2 Combine the nibbles to make the binary number.

10100110

A6 is equivalent to 10100110.

BINARY REPRESENTATION
OF CHARACTERS, IMAGES & SOUND

CHARACTERS

Computers can only understand and process binary data. As a result, they need to be able to convert characters to binary data and vice versa.

A character set is the complete set of characters used by a computer and is created through encoding each character with a unique code or value.

Different character sets can contain different amounts of characters.

3 Computer converts code into character for display or print

2 Binary code sent to computer

1 Button pressed on keyboard

The ASCII (American Standard Code for Information Interchange) character set uses numbers 0 to 127 to represent characters.

To store 128 different character codes, a 7-bit binary code is required.

Character	Binary	Hex	Denary
A	01000001	41	65
a	01100001	61	97
G	01000111	47	71
4	00110100	34	52
'space'	00100000	20	32

Since the smallest size representation on most computers is a byte (8 bits), a 0 is added to the start of each 7 bit binary code to make a full byte.

To accommodate new characters, such as non-English characters, ASCII was extended to an 8-bit binary code, which allowed for an additional 128 characters.

Unicode is a character set that uses 16-bit or 32-bit binary codes to represent characters. This allows for over one million different characters and symbols.

SOUND

Sound is made when something vibrates, creating waves. Sound waves are analogue; this means that they change continuously and do not have a measurable value.

Computers cannot understand analogue data, so it must be converted to discrete digital data using a method called 'sampling'.

In sampling, the amplitude of the analogue sound wave is sampled at set intervals and the values are then recorded digitally.

Digital Sound
Analogue Sound

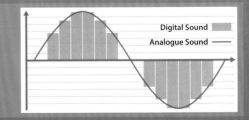

daydream EDUCATION

IMAGES

Images are made up of pixels (the smallest possible coloured dot on a computer screen). An image made up of pixels is called a 'bitmap image'.

This very simple image shows how pixels are made up of binary code. The digit 0 is used for white and the digit 1 is used for black.

In reality, images are a lot more complex than the smiley face example shown, with colour depth and resolution having a big impact on the quality and file size of an image.

Colour Depth

To be able to represent more than two colours in an image each pixel requires more bits. The number of bits used for each pixel is known as colour depth.

A 1-bit image can display 2^1, or 2 colours.

A 2-bit image can display 2^2, or 4 colours.

A 4-bit image can display 2^4, or 16 colours.

A 16-bit image can display 2^{16}, or 65536 colours.

16-bit Image   2-bit Image

300 dpi

72 dpi

Resolution

Resolution is the number of dots or pixels per linear unit (usually dots per inch – dpi). The greater the resolution of an image, the greater the quality and file size.

Images also include metadata that provides the computer with more information about the image, enabling the computer to recreate the image from the binary data in the file. Metadata often includes details such as the file format, pixel height and width, colour depth and resolution.

The number of times the sound level is sampled per second is called the 'sampling frequency'. A typical sampling frequency is 44,100 times per second (44.1 kHz).

Sample size, or bit depth, is the number of bits used to store each sample. Bit depth is measured in binary digits (bits) and for every 1-bit increase, the accuracy is doubled.

Bit rate is the number of bits used per second to store each sample. It is measured in kilobits per second (kbps) and can be calculated using the following formula:

Bit rate = sample frequency × sample size

The higher the bit rate (sample frequency and sample size) of an audio recording, the better the quality. However, as bit rate increases so does file size.

UNITS OF INFORMATION & DATA COMPRESSION

Computers cannot process analogue data. As a result, analogue data must be converted to digital data (binary code) before it can be processed.

BINARY DATA

Binary data consists of two distinct values: 0s and 1s. Off or false is represented by 0 and on or true is represented by 1. A single binary digit (0 or 1) is called a 'bit'.

┌1 bit (b)┐				├──────── 1 nibble ────────┤			
1	0	1	0	0	0	1	0

└──────────────────── 1 byte (B) ────────────────────┘

Quantities of bytes can be described using decimal prefixes which represent powers of 10.

Prefix	Name	Abbreviation	Size
kilo (10^3)	Kilobyte	kB	1,000 bytes
mega (10^6)	Megabyte	MB	1,000 kilobytes
giga (10^9)	Gigabyte	GB	1,000 megabytes
tera (10^{12})	Terabyte	TB	1,000 gigabytes
peta (10^{15})	Petabyte	PB	1,000 terabytes

DATA COMPRESSION

Data files can be compressed to reduce download times and storage requirements.

Lossy Compression

In lossy compression data is permanently removed from a file to reduce its size.

- Reduces file size significantly
- Reduces the quality of original file
- Not suitable for text files or computer programs that must retain all original data
- Removed data cannot be restored

Original Image   Reduced Quality Image

Example file types: JPEG, MP3, MPEG-4.

Lossless Compression

In lossless compression no data is removed. Redundant and duplicate data is repurposed to reduce file size.

- Less file-size reduction than with lossy compression
- Decompresses back to original quality
- Can be used on computer programs and text files

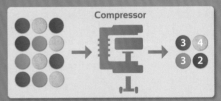

Example file types: PNG, TIFF, ZIP.

daydream
EDUCATION